Other Worlds

Other Worlds:
The Fantasy Genre

John H. Timmerman

Bowling Green University Popular Press
Bowling Green, Ohio 43403

CONTENTS

CHAPTER ONE
  INTRODUCTION   1

CHAPTER TWO
  STORY   5

CHAPTER THREE
  CHARACTER   29

CHAPTER FOUR
  ANOTHER WORLD   49

CHAPTER FIVE
  MAGIC AND THE SUPERNATURAL:
  GOOD AND EVIL   72

CHAPTER SIX
  THE QUEST   91

CHAPTER SEVEN
  A CONTEMPORARY FANTASY: THE CHRONICLES OF
  THOMAS COVENANT, UNBELIEVER   103

NOTES   116

INDEX   123

Chapter One

Introduction

In "Birches," Robert Frost looks upon the ice-bowed branches of the pliant birch and imagines a boy swinging upon them. Trusting to his imagination and materials at hand, the boy turns momentarily from this world to the free swing of the birch bough. "It's when I'm weary of considerations," writes Frost, "And life is too much like a pathless wood," that he too finds himself longing "to get away from earth awhile." Frost immediately qualifies his longing:

> May no fate willfully misunderstand me
> And half grant what I wish and snatch me away
> Not to return. Earth's the right place for love....

That affirmation lies at the heart of fantasy literature; the reader longs to stand apart for a time, not to escape but to rejoin earth's "pathless wood" with a clearer sense of direction and purpose. Fantasy is essentially rejuvenative. It permits us a certain distance from pragmatic affairs and offers us a far clearer insight into them.

This fact may account, in part, for the enormous appeal of fantasy literature. It does more than simply restructure a reality which we already know—it also offers a parallel reality which gives us a renewed awareness of what we already know. There is an enormous and unquenchable thirst in humankind for precisely this opportunity for pause. And, as the pace of modern life inexorably quickens, the fascination for fantasy literature quickens simultaneously.

"A child," J.R.R. Tolkien once wrote, "may well believe a report that there are ogres in the next country; many grown-up persons find it easy to believe of another country."[1] Here is the invitation fantasy extends to the reader—to recover a belief which has been beclouded by knowledge, to renew a faith which has been shattered by fact. We may *know* there are no ogres in the

1

next country—we haven't seen them in our travels—yet we may well *believe* there are. Like other types of literature, fantasy gives us the opportunity to become lost for a time in another world so that we can discover or recover a fresh perspective in this world. Bruno Bettelheim acknowledges this in his study of fairy tales, *The Uses of Enchantment:* "If we hope to live not just from moment to moment, but in true consciousness of our existence, then our greatest need and most difficult achievement is to find meaning in our lives. It is well known how many have lost the will to live, and have stopped trying, because such meaning has evaded them."[2]

Fantasy is not a new thing under the sun, after all. Its legitimate forebears include the fairy tale, the Romance, and the fable. But man's thirst for "otherness" has sharpened in recent decades. A casual glance at booksellers' lists will disclose the phenomenal surge in sales figures for fantasy works.[3] More startling, perhaps, is the fact that these works are not only sold but read.

As fantasy literature has become increasingly popular, more critical attention has been paid to it. For some years this attention was professionally coordinated by scholarly organizations such as The Popular Culture Association of America. Within the last few years several books on fantasy have been published by major presses. These books share two common traits. First, they generally focus on individual authors and individual fantasy works. Primary attention goes to certain works worthy of that attention by virtue of their aesthetic merit. This is a worthwhile and necessary endeavor, but it does little to identify the unique properties of the genre itself. There is little critical distinction, for example, between fantasy and its related genres such as science fiction. Second, but akin to the first, is the common failure to identify fantasy's place in the tradition of western literature. What features does fantasy share with all outstanding literature? Fantasy is not a sideshow at a shady corner of the main thoroughfare. Although unique, and deserving of individual identification as a genre, fantasy has a central place in the western tradition as a whole. It provides new ways of seeing a thing, and new answers to what is seen; but it deals with enduring matters.

The task now seems to be one of identifying the genre and locating its relation to literary tradition. There are attendant questions: What is the worth of fantasy? What does it do? Why and how does it do what it does? Such questions may be answered only by a thorough consideration of the primary issue.

It may be precisely in defiance of such theorizing that fantasy exists. Some readers have observed that J.R.R. Tolkien really had a critic in mind when he wrote:

> But harder than stone is the flesh and bone
> Of a troll that sits in the hills alone.

Fantasy seeks the undefinable; its subject is nothing less than the human spirit. This, in part, accounts for its powerful impact. Fantasy is never content with objective testimony to pragmatic reality; instead, it explores the world of humankind in its spiritual reality. Ursula K. Le Guin has commented that "A fantasy is a journey. It is a journey into the subconscious mind, just as psychoanalysis is. Like psychoanalysis, it can be dangerous; *and it will change you.*"[5]

All the more important, then, is the need for a better understanding of the genre. In *A Preface to Paradise Lost* C.S. Lewis states that "The first qualification for judging any piece of workmanship from a corkscrew to a cathedral is to know *what* it is—what it was intended to do and how it was meant to be used... the first thing is to understand the object before you...."[6] But form is not always easy to understand. As Lewis might have pointed out, some cathedrals may look like overblown corkscrews, and it is possible to imagine a corkscrew having a steeple-shaped handle. Form is always something intensely individual for the creative artist; no less so than his ideas. Somehow, within established literary patterns he must find an individual pattern which may be shaped to best reveal what he has to say. As Lewis suggests, "The matter inside the poet *wants* the Form: in submitting to the Form it becomes really original, really the origin of great work."[7]

My intention here is not to craft one more paean to the expert authors of fantasy literature we now have, a task that has been undertaken admirably by several scholars. My concern instead is to understand the form that the fantasy writer *wants*, and in fact achieves. The effort here is to attempt a theoretical understanding of why fantasy operates, how it operates, and to what end it operates by focusing upon the nature of the genre itself.

Like most readers of fantasy literature, I have been

enchanted by certain authors. I was tempted to turn repeatedly to those authors for evidence, but I have resisted that temptation insofar as possible. When individual examples were called for, I attempted to select them from fairly well-known works.

In this study I will identify six traits which must be present *to some degree* to characterize the work as fantasy literature. In each instance I have attempted to use the common literary terms, although fantasy literature may make special use of those terms. These six traits are the use of traditional *Story*, the depiction of *Common Characters and Heroism,* the evocation of *Another World,* the employment of *Magic and the Supernatural,* the revelation of a *Struggle between Good and Evil,* and the tracing of a *Quest.* By understanding these theoretical qualities of fantasy, perhaps we can discern that the sideshow does indeed belong center stage, taking its proper place in the literary tradition.

In John Gardner's *Grendel,* the uncanny monster is reminded that "Tedium is the worst pain." Perhaps we shall look at more theorizing at first than fantasy, but it is only to permit us to exclaim with another voice that Grendel hears: *"The gods made this world for our joy!"* Grendel reflects: "The people listen to him dutifully, heads bowed. It does not impress them, one way or the other, that he's crazy."[8] The question is whether we can provide the theoretical structures that permit us to make that happy claim without Grendel's final qualifying clause.

Chapter Two

Story

It seems obvious that fantasy relies upon a compelling, well-paced story, but this fact is often overlooked or obscured. It is overlooked when one considers the work simply as a springboard to allegorical meanings, and is obscured when one does not distinguish fantasy from related genres. In its traditional sense, *story* requires a narrative plot line, the unfolding of events, the development of characters into living beings who think about actions, who do act, and whose actions have effects. A story moves from a beginning, through a middle, to an end, and in the process emotionally or psychologically moves the reader. Story, considered within these boundaries, is a structure with a purpose and end.

A good story has always been the foremost aim of fantasists. Reflecting on *The Chronicles of Narnia,* C.S. Lewis admitted that "I fell in love with the Form [of fantasy] itself; its brevity, its severe restraints on description, its flexible traditionalism, its inflexible hostility to all analysis, digression, reflections and 'gas'."[1] This central focus upon story does not mean that fantasy authors condemn themselves to sterile prose. Quite the opposite is true, but story is always the central pole about which aesthetic excellences such as internal richness, complication, imagery, and harmony may revolve. The centrality of story does at once separate fantasy from several allied genres, but also locates the genre in relation to them and literary tradition. This may be seen by considering fantasy in relation to three related genres; allegory, science fiction, and dystopian literature.

Fantasy and Allegory

Like all great works of literature, both allegory and fantasy suggest meanings which arise from story but lie beyond the story. Where do such meanings lie? In the minds of the readers. Because of the suggestive nature of the two genres, one would expect to

5

find them comfortably allied. Yet, fantasy authors have been adamant, even strident at times, in their opposition to calling their work allegory. We deal here with an uncomfortable position in critical analysis; a respect for the author's *intentions*, the nature of the work itself, and the reaction to the work by readers. Clearly, the most legitimate area for critical scrutiny, as Brooks and Warren insisted, is the second. Mindful of their dictates, however, we are compelled to consider all three areas to arrive at some clear distinctions in this particular case. As a frame of reference we remind ourselves of C. Hugh Holman's accurate and sufficient definition of allegory:

> A form of extended metaphor in which objects and persons in a narrative, either in prose or verse, are equated with meanings that lie outside the narrative itself. Thus it represents one thing in the guise of another—an abstraction in that of a concrete image.... Allegory attempts to evoke a dual interest, one in the events, characters, and setting presented, and the other in the ideas they are intended to convey or the significance they bear.[2]

It is the kind of story, as Peter Schakel argues in *Reading with the Heart,* to be read with the head, with all intellectual faculties geared to the machinations of the developing metaphor. In contrast, fantasy story is meant to be read first with the heart.[3]

As a general premise we should agree that Story seeks to free the imagination, to allow the imagination to live for a time in another world. This would be true of all great literature. In allegory the *author* deliberately patterns the fictional world in order to suggest specific meanings to the reader. To be successful, the allegorical *work* must be self-restrictive; that is to say, a figure who on page one represents death may not on page ten represent life. Moving without variation from the plane of the narrative to the plane of pre-set allegorical meaning, the story is essentially two-dimensional. The task of the *reader* is to establish this two-dimensional parallelism. The matter is one of puzzle-solving, of arranging the pieces within its narrative form. The reader, however, is completing someone else's puzzle. He may take a certain pleasure in that task, but allegory provides within its own framework its own solution.

Fantasy supplies several variations to this. First, we must recognize the *authors'* repeated protests against reading their work as allegorical. Ursula K. Le Guin, who started her career in science fiction before finding her *metier* in fantasy, is emphatic in her distaste for allegory: "I hate allegories. A is 'really' B, and a hawk is 'really' a handsaw—bah. Humbug. Any creation, primary or secondary, with any vitality to it, can 'really' be a dozen mutually exclusive things at once, before breakfast."[4] J.R.R. Tolkien was similarly emphatic on the issue. In the Foreword to *The Lord of the Rings,* Tolkien wrote:

> I cordially dislike allegory in all its manifestations, and always have done so since I grew old and ware enough to detect its presence. I much prefer history, true or feigned, with its varied applicability to the thought and experience of readers. I think that many confuse 'applicability' with 'allegory'; but the one resides in the freedom of the reader, and the other in the purposed domination of the author.[5]

Tolkien also commented that "The prime motive was the desire of a tale-teller to try his hand at a really long story that would hold the attention of readers, amuse them, delight them, and at times maybe excite them or deeply move them."[6] The statements are critical to understanding story. Story lives on in the reader; it becomes the reader's history and spiritual domain. In each instance, Le Guin and Tolkien, the author's dissatisfaction with allegory resides in its rigidity of *form* which makes the story merely a handmaiden to *Meanings*. Story, they insist, has intrinsic worth. Its tone, feeling, suggestiveness work as strongly on the reader as any deliberately staged symbolic references.

But story also has purpose. The *reader* may see things *by means of it*. In a discussion of Tolkien's work, William Ready comments that "There is one real purpose in Story: to reveal a truth by a tale, a tale that can be read for itself with enjoyment and yet where, upon reflection—which may or may not come—Truth enters in, often as unwelcome and forbidding as a creed."[7] Consider also C.S. Lewis's comment in a letter to Peter Milward: "What you would call 'a pleasant story for the children' would be to him [Tolkien] more serious than an allegory."[8] Lewis continued with an explicit distinction between story and allegory: "My view would be that a good myth (i.e. a story out of which ever varying meanings will grow for different readers and in different ages) is a higher thing than an allegory (into which *one* meaning has been put). Into an allegory a man can put only what he already knows; in a myth he puts what he does not yet know and could not come by any other way."[9]

On the one hand, then, we observe a disinclination among fantasists to label their work as allegory. Yet they are emphatic in their belief that story suggests meanings to its audience. The pattern of allegory is preset by the author, and its ultimate success rests upon the reader's perception of the exact interrelationship between a symbol in the story and its place on a plane of meaning. Story in fantasy operates quite differently in that it is open-ended. All story, as I point out in the concluding section of this chapter, has meaning. But in fantasy, meaning is *appropriated* by the reader rather than *given* by the author. We may borrow a theological term here and describe what is appropriated as *anagogic insight*—an immediate apprehension of spiritual patterns which has been stimulated by certain literary figures, symbols, or devices.

By careful construction of the story, the fantasy author suggests certain anagoges. By repetition of pointing signals, or symbols, the author constructs a pattern which guides the interpretation. But in no sense does the writer force the pattern upon the reader. The reader, by following the pattern, claims the anagogic insight as his own. The story becomes his own story to the extent that his imagination interpenetrates the framework of the story and lives for a time in the world of the story. The insights thereby disclosed to one reader may vary from those disclosed to another reader by virtue of the degree of interpenetration. One symbol may affect one reader more powerfully than it would another reader. Similarly, one reader may take from the story insights not apparent to another reader. Thus the pattern is dynamic and varying. It should be pointed out that this is precisely what Lewis desired in his use of mythic, fantasy literature. In a review of Tolkien's *Fellowship of the Ring,* Lewis claimed that "What shows that we are reading myth, not allegory, is that there are no pointers to a specifically theological, or political, or psychological application. A myth points, for each reader, to the realm he lives in most. It is a master key; use it on what door you like."[10] Clearly, every author provides paths toward certain such doors, but the reader finally opens them. By my term "anagogic insight" I mean precisely the way in which the reader uses the master-keys of the story to unlock ever-varying personal doors in his own life. In allegory there is one door, although different readers may find it more or less exciting and satisfying to enter. In fantasy there are finally as many doors as there are readers.

A qualification is in order here, however. Allegory as a literary form is not intrinsically less valuable than fantasy.

Fantasy is related to allegory in the sense that all great literature lives on in the reader, and carries special import beyond the written page. This is a quality of story anywhere. The distinction in this case is the special insistence with which fantasy authors consider this power of suggestiveness.

J.R.R. Tolkien's fear of allegory is that it will confine and compress the work. Yet, his marvellous short story "Leaf by Niggle" clearly partakes of allegorical elements. Certain "stock characters" of the allegorical tradition enter the tale at the author's deliberate will. Perhaps because of his own scholarly work in the Anglo-Saxon mystery poems, which partake of standard symbolic structures that suggest something beyond the structures themselves, Tolkien insists upon a suggestiveness beyond the allegorical features of this short story. If Tolkien constructed his own theory of fantasy in "On Fairy Stories," a theory discussed in Chapter Four of this study, then "Leaf by Niggle" is a fictional counterpart to the theory. The tale is a clear and deliberate effort to incarnate a theory in fiction.

First written in 1939 and published in 1945, the story was initially read by its first slim audience as a statement about World War II, particularly in the harsh pragmatism of Councillor Tompkins at the story's conclusion. Similar readings have of course been given to *The Lord of the Rings*. The blood-thirsty Orcs, for example, have been construed as the Nazi regime. And in *The Hobbit* the goblins' fascination with war mechanism has similarly been read as applicable to Nazi fanaticism. There is a strong possibility of that, of course, in descriptions such as this from *The Hobbit*:

> Goblins are cruel, wicked, and bad-hearted. They make no beautiful things, but they make many clever ones.... It is not unlikely that they invented some of the machines that have since troubled the world, especially the ingenious devices for killing large numbers of people at once, for wheels and engines and explosions always delighted them, and also not working with their own hands more than they could help....[11]

Tolkien's worry, I believe, is that we *limit* his stories to this. He might say instead that World War II is a particular manifestation of evil which has occurred in all tribes and tongues and occurs also in fantasy. But we may not limit the full meaning of fantasy to that alone. If we do, if we see Tolkien as allegorist, we see in his fiction essentially a negative picture and a series of indictments.

If we see him as fantasist, as he insisted we do, then we see characters led through trials in evil to ultimate joy. The effect, then, and the total picture are positive in tone. This distinction may be made clearer by considering "Leaf by Niggle" as fantasy, if we attempt in the consideration to separate those individual structures which may be called "allegorical" from the total effect of the story.

Niggle is a nondescript little man, one who in this story has a long journey to make. Typically Tolkien's characters are not initially excited about the journeys they have to make. They are quite content where they are. And Niggle's particular contentment is painting, which he does as he is able to find time and not very successfully at that. He is a common man, "kind-hearted in a way." Tolkien makes him familiar to us. "You know the sort of kind heart," he adds. And so we share some of Niggle's annoyance at the prospect of the journey. Much preferable, it would seem to us, to give the old gentleman some leisure to paint. Particularly this one painting he has labored over so long:

> It had begun with a leaf caught in the wind, and it became a tree; and the tree grew, sending out innumerable branches, and thrusting out the most fantastic roots. Strange birds came and settled on the twigs and had to be attended to. Then all round the Tree, and behind it, through the gaps in the leaves and boughs, a country began to open out; and there were glimpses of a forest marching over the land, and of mountains tipped with snow.[12]

Perhaps it would be better for Niggle if he were less kind-hearted, for people continually interrupt him. And always there is that prospect of the unspecified "long journey," for which Niggle desultorily does a bit of packing now and then.

The primary culprit in Niggle's interruptions is a crotchety neighbor named Parish. Parish is oblivious to the intricacies of Niggle's marvelous painting. He is, in fact, an aesthetic philistine; hard-nosed, pragmatic, and always interrupting. It would not take a very keen wit to begin to construe the allegorical context established here—a man possessed with finding his life's work; the sense that the work is but an adumbration of some more concrete, divine reality; a long journey to make at an unspecified but imminently expected time; a series of interruptions from those about him in his "parish" that prevent him from completion of his life's task. We are not surprised then when Niggle suddenly is stricken with fever and is paid a visit by the literary archetype of the mysterious stranger who prefigures death, "a tall man" and "a total stranger." And close on his heels is his double, a man "dressed all in black."

The second stranger, like Emily Dickinson's figure in "Because I could not stop for Death—/He kindly stopped for me," arrives with Niggle's carriage. He is transported to a train station for the longer trip and along the way "Niggle was feeling very tired and sleepy." The train he boards "ran almost at once into a dark tunnel." If the pattern is still uncertain, Tolkien provides clear allegorical landmarks as Niggle spends time in a purgatorial half-way house—"He was never allowed outside, and the windows all looked inward"—and is called to do certain tasks of penance. Here, however, occurs the first suggestion of Tolkien's subtle shift into fantasy. Thus far he has worked solidly in traditional allegorical form. Each step in the "earthly" story is precisely patterned to an equivalent "heavenly" or abstract story. But, curiously, in purgatory Niggle performs tasks which are better suited to Parish. Why these tasks, he wonders. And the reader begins to wonder with him. Something here is stretching suggestively beyond pure allegory. We can find no touchstone in our "earthly" story by which to establish the succeeding actions.

It would seem, however, that for a moment we are solidly back in allegory when Niggle's case is heard before a kind of "Court of Inquiry." There the First Voice, the Accuser or God as upholder of Old Testament law, and The Second Voice, the Advocate or Jesus as New Testament grace, debate Niggle's case. The Second Voice prevails in its plea that: "It is a case for a little gentle treatment now." In response:

> Niggle thought that he had never heard anything so generous as that Voice. It made Gentle Treatment sound like a load of rich gifts, and the summons to a King's feast. (p. 101)

This is the point where allegory would end, with the invitation to the "marriage feast of the lamb." Indeed, this is where allegory must end, for the symbolic frame of reference has been exhausted in the story. We have no earthly parallel for the events that follow. Niggle is permitted into heaven, but it is a fantastic heaven, full of surprise and wonder that transcend the parallel dimensions of allegory. Riding his bicycle (of all things) into heaven's splendor, Niggle observes that:

> It was green and close; and yet he could see every blade distinctly. He

seemed to remember having seen or dreamed of that sweep of grass
somewhere or other. The curves of the land were familiar somehow.
Yes: the ground was becoming level, as it should, and now, of course,
it was beginning to rise again. A great green shadow came between
him and the sun. Niggle looked up, and fell off his bicycle.
Before him stood the Tree, his Tree, finished. (p. 103)

This for Tolkien is what fairy story does: it leads us by imperfect leaves, bits and pieces of imaginative insight, into a glimpse of the Tree, the perfect whole. "It's a gift!" Niggle exclaims. Nothing more nor less. This imaginative vision cannot be structured or regimented. The insight into wholeness comes like a gift. The result of seeing the tree for Niggle is the gaining of a clearer view: "After a time Niggle turned towards the Forest. Not because he was tired of the Tree, but he seemed to have got it all clear in his mind now, and was aware of it, and of its growth, even when he was not looking at it" (p. 104). Yet, he is surprised to meet his old neighbor Parish there. In fact, Parish has been at work on the tree. While Niggle has learned order, Parish has learned wonder:

As they worked together, it became plain that Niggle was now the
better of the two at ordering his time and getting things done. Oddly
enough, it was Niggle who became most absorbed in building and
gardening, while Parish often wandered about looking at trees, and
especially at the Tree. (p. 106)

Niggle and Parish spend pleasant days here before a shepherd comes to guide them to the mountains, a symbol here for Tolkien, as it always was for his friend C.S. Lewis, of "Deep Heaven." We leave Niggle and parish making that trip.

The supreme touch of this happy little story, however, is that Tolkien takes us back to earth. It is the world we, the readers, have to return to, and we find in this world Councillor Tompkins and others debating Niggle's peculiar case: " 'I think he was a silly little man,' said Councillor Tompkins. 'Worthless, in fact; no use to Society at all!' " (p. 110). This is the world of pragmatic and practical measurements for "use" that we find ourselves in. Tolkien questions whether we can nonetheless glimpse the joy of Niggle. And the last line belongs to Niggle and parish: "They both laughed. Laughed—the Mountains rang with it."

While allegory and fantasy enjoy a familiar relationship, we see nonetheless that they are separated by the special insistence by fantasy authors that their work be open-ended, suggestively stirring "anagogic insights" rather than exactly parallel patterns in the minds of readers. The difference is one of tone and emphasis. A similar distinction comes to bear on fantasy and science fiction.

Fantasy and Science Fiction

Exploring the distinctions between fantasy and science fiction is equivalent to marking differences in identical twins. There are many similarities, yet the different names call forth different beings. Each answers to its own name. The fact that both have been assimilated under a common rubric, like twins sharing a surname, has not eased the difficulty.

According to Sam J. Lundwall, in *Science Fiction: An Illustrated History,* "The term 'science fiction' was first coined in 1851 by the British essayist William Wilson, in *A Little Ernest Book Upon a Great Old Subject.*"[13] For Wilson, science fiction was little more than "the revealed truths of Science...interwoven with a pleasing story which may itself be poetical and true...."[14] The history is a bit more convoluted, since Wilson's concept was antedated by the French *Voyages Imaginaires* of 1787-89. But there is a "newness" about science fiction that separates it from the fantasy tradition rooted in the fairy tale and the romance. It is a difference of tenor and approach and aim.

It should be easy to distinguish between realism and science fiction. Many readers are rightfully nervous about this distinction, however. What is realism? For matters at hand, I am considering it in its traditional literary sense and no other. It is a tradition which rooted in Aristotelian *mimesis,* which blossomed in 18th century empiricism, and which flowered in naturalistic fidelity to life as it is observed. This is the realism of Zola, Stephen Crane, Robbe-Grillet, and a few thousand modern novels. Darko Suvin has chosen to define science fiction by redefining realism: "SF is, then, a literary genre whose necessary and sufficient conditions are the presence and interaction of estrangement and cognition, and whose main formal device is an imaginative framework alternative to the author's empirical environment."[15] Essentially, we mean the same thing.

While they share much in common when set against realism, science fiction and fantasy are distinctly different. The following points may be observed.

1. *Dependence on technological instruments*

Essential to science fiction are scientific or technological instruments. This basic premise is still the watershed distinction between science fiction and fantasy. For example, science fiction often translates a character to another world, but arrival at this other world is *always dependent* upon a scientific or technological device. Fantasy *may* make use of a device for translation to another world, but it is usually a magical device such as an amulet, a ring, or a sacred word. Quite often no such device is used but the other world is evoked whole in itself. The characters and readers are simply there.

The central concern in science fiction, however, remains decidedly the effects of science on man. Ben Bova observes that "Perhaps this is the ultimate role of science fiction: to act as an interpreter of science to humanity.... Only knowledgeable people can wisely decide how to use science and technoloy for humankind's benefit."[16] Without science and technology as central factors, science fiction could not exist.

2. Suspension of disbelief

This point follows directly upon the first. Science fiction would have the reader believe that given certain scientific or technological devices—a space ship, a time device, a special fuel—it is *possible* to arrive at this other world. But we have to suspend our disbelief—that is, set aside our knowledge that there does not now exist such a space ship—before we believe in the possibility. Fantasy simply asks us to believe *we* are in this other world. Given certain geographical or other physical traits of such a world, it is a probable world.

3. Projection

Science fiction is frequently set in the future, and has often been called "futuristic" fiction. It is interested in the effects of science and technology on man in a future state. While projection should be distinguished from prediction, it remains a central scheme in the tapestry of science fiction. Sam Lundwall writes:

Science fiction does not predict the future, except accidentally. It extrapolates, it amplifies, it magnifies. It deals with changes, the inventions of a scientific, social or political nature that inevitably must change our world whether we like it or not. How we will react to those changes, and how they will affect our lives, *that* is the rub.[17]

Ben Bova goes further in his belief that science fiction holds open as many futures as possible for man: "Science fiction writers are not in the business of predicting *the* future. They do something much more important. They try to show the many possible futures that lie open to us."[18] The common denominator of these definitions is the orientation to the future, the foreseeing capacity of science fiction for the possible effects of science and technology upon man, or, as Mark Rose writes, "the taste, the feel, the human meaning of scientific discoveries."[19]

Fantasy, on the contrary, calls forth a wholly other world. Since it is not predicated upon our world except by spiritual realities, fantasy is timeless and enduring. C. N. Manlove has argued that while science fiction is a projection of our world, if fantasy takes place in our world it is juxtaposed to it. There is what Manlove calls a "diametric reversal."[20] The wholly other world of fantasy cannot be overtaken except by the imagination.

Fantasy, Science Fiction, and Dystopian Literature

It is on this issue of projection, or "extrapolation" as it is often called in science fiction criticism, that science fiction shares an affinity with dystopian fiction, for dystopian fiction looks into the future to reveal a way we should not go. The term "utopia" is a play on the Greek *eu-topia*, a word carrying the etymological meaning of "a good place." Utopia borrows the negative prefix *u* to suggest "no place." A utopia is, then, a good place which is no place, a thoroughly imaginary world. And a dystopia is a thoroughly bad place projected into the future but predicated on events currently occuring on our place.

Science fiction handles its projected world in two ways. One might be called "space" fiction, which is predicated upon another world with vaguely familiar scientific trappings such as interstellar travel, technological mechanisms such as robots or lasars or computers, or various chemical concoctions that prolong, destroy, or simply attenuate life. The other type of science fiction is predicated upon our world but projects it into foreseen events or timespans. The latter would include dystopian fiction. There is a danger in this projection. While the author might revel in the unfolding reality of his vision in *our* time, such fiction is essentially anachronistic. Fifty years ago science fiction projected its other world as the moon, but its world was framed into our reality as we voyaged to the moon. Twenty years ago the projection was on Mars. Now we in fact know a great deal about Mars and might not be inclined to travel there even should the opportunity be provided. It has become a part of our world. Science fiction continually runs the risk of being overtaken by the very science it projects.

Dystopian literature, since it projects our world into the future, runs the same risk of being overtaken by time. But with dystopian literature the theme is basically the timeless nature of man's spirit. It is less susceptible to anachronism than projective science fiction because the scientific accoutrements of its futuristic world are not of immediate importance. For example, the scientific mechanism of Bokanovsky's Process in *Brave New World* is less important than the fact that the Process is a mode of genetic engineering which we do now, in fact, have with us. This problem of future worlds and present meanings may be seen clearly in three prominent contemporary works of dystopian literature.

Aldous Huxley's *Brave New World* ranks, with the possible exception of Orwell's 1984, as the most significant dystopian work of our time. Huxley's stated aim in the novel is to shock us into an awareness that technological gadgetry is enslaving us in a world of self-appeasement. John Savage, Huxley's alter-ego in the novel, utters Huxley's battle cry in an important dialogue with Mustapha Mond:

> 'In fact,' said Mustapha Mond, 'you're claiming the right to be unhappy.'
> 'All right then,' said the Savage defiantly, 'I'm claiming the right to be unhappy.'
> 'Not to mention the right to grow old and ugly and impotent; the right to have syphilis and cancer; the right to have too little to eat; the right to be lousy; the right to live in constant apprehension of what may happen tomorrow; the right to catch typhoid; the right to be tortured by unspeakable pains of every kind.' There was a long silence.
> 'I claim them all,' said the Savage at last.[21]

The Savage claims all these, for they are a small expense for human freedom, and the human dignity which cannot exist apart from that freedom.

It is true, in a sense, that Huxley's novel shares the danger of anachronism. The terror of Bokanovsky's Process is commonplace in our genetic laboratories, and because commonplace it is no longer terrible. The counter-culture radicals of the 1960s had strawberry soma, except they called it LSD. Yet Huxley warns us what we stand to lose in the unchecked path of

Scientism, the worship of Scientific method as a god unto itself. Dystopian literature tells us what we are in danger of losing; and perhaps Huxley's novel tells us what we have already lost. Like fantasy, it helps us understand where we are by being elsewhere, in the brave new world, for a time. In "A Reading of *Brave New World:* Dystopianism in Historical Perspective," W. Andrew Hoffecker has ably located Huxley in the broad sweep of the western history of ideas. Hoffecker writes:

Dystopian authors are far more than doomsday prophets. They warn about what society might realistically become not so much from *default* or the absence of societal planning, but from the very success of societal plans conceived on the basis of false views of man. They oppose the designs of men whose goal is to mold man into patterns which would dehumanize him.[22]

Hoffecker goes on to demonstrate how in *Brave New World* "We find a society in which Plato's 'Good has gone Bad,' Augustine's 'Heavenly city is perverted and secularized,' and Roger Williams' 'Liberty of conscience is imprisoned.' "[23] For Huxley, the past holds within it the secret of our future survival. If we choose to entomb the past, as the World Controllers of the brave new world have done, we have thereby also entombed our future. This dual concept—the menace of Scientism and the failure to learn from the past—figures prominently in two later dystopian works, Arthur C. Clarke's *Childhood's End* and Walter Miller's *A Canticle for Leibowitz.*

In *Childhood's End,* Arthur Clarke, well-known for his science fiction, engages more nearly dystopian literature by virtue of his careful critique of science itself. Science fiction traditionally has one of two attitudes toward science; it either uses science as a vehicle for an interstellar, futuristic adventure, or it glories in the paraphernalia of science itself. Seldom does it hold science up to serious critique. Clark's *Childhood's End* is as much about science itself as it is about the Overlords' threat to the fictional world. The Overlords are threatening *because* of their advanced scientific achievement, and *because* the humans in the story have given them unlicensed freedom to exercise it.

The story has some elements commonly associated with fantasy. It uses, for example, the power of magic in an Ouija game and in the preternatural prescience of certain characters. But this magic is limited precisely by the hard, mechanical knowledge of the Overlords.

In the novel we are placed in a futuristic (not wholly other) world in which the space visitors, the Overlords, have brought an unmitigated stability. " 'Let me ask you a few questions,' " says Stormgren, leader of the Freedom League of Nations, " 'Can you deny that the Overlords have brought security, peace, and prosperity to the world?' "[24] The response is this: " 'But they have taken our liberty.... Freedom to control our own lives, under God's guidance' " (p.16). We have, then, a conflict similar to Huxley's *Brave New World* and to all dystopian literature: for the security which the power of science affords we have sacrificed individual, human freedom. The problem endures; how much freedom does one give up in order to acquire security?

In this world of *Childhood's End* there are those who, in answer to that question, are willing to say: not much. Human freedom is more precious than absolute rule, even with attendant risks. Underground movements are at work in this world. But their power is feeble, and that is precisely the issue. The Overlords have unrelenting *power*; power which strips man spiritually naked of his hopes, his dreams, his myths, his childhood. Stormgren reflects on Karellen, the name given to the mysterious Overlord:

> ... Were *you* the one who failed, before the dawn of human history? It must have been a failure indeed, thought Stormgren, for its echoes to roll down all the ages, to haunt the childhood of every race of man. Even in fifty years, could you overcome the power of all the myths and legends of the world? (p. 64)

For fifty years the Overlords are permitted to exercise their power, and "Fifty years is ample time in which to change a world and its people almost beyond recognition. All that is required for the task are a sound knowledge of social engineering, a clear sight of the intended goal—and power" (p. 69). Like the World Controllers in *Brave New World,* the Overlords believe that in simple power lies the key to all human difficulties: "Though their goal was hidden, their knowledge was obvious—and so was their power" (p. 69). Perhaps this is true; but what then of man? That is the question of Clarke's novel. Having become mere pawns, stripped of childhood wonder, imagination, and stories, reduced to a tamed domesticity, do we have any humankind at all? Perhaps not; but we have in this story unvarying peace: "By the standards of all earlier ages, it was Utopia. Ignorance, disease, poverty, and fear had virtually ceased to exist. The memory of war was fading into the past as a nightmare vanishes with the dawn; soon it would lie outside the experience of all living men" (p. 71). The situation is a close copy of that brave new world created by Mustapha Mond and his World Controllers.

Like Aldous Huxley, Clarke examines his futuristic world and finds it wanting. Power is assimilated into one place and the reader is not surprised in *Childhood's End* to find that power personified as the Devil: "There was no mistake. The leathery wings, the little horns, the barbed tail—all were there" (p. 69). Also like Huxley, Clarke examines the effects of this world upon science. He finds that when the world is stripped of wonder and religion, science degenerates. The trade-off for pure science—free, uninhibited research—is mere technology, or what C.S. Lewis called Scientism. Technology, to the minds of Clarke or Huxley, is something mandated. It is a slave to the age, trying with rapid deployment forces of scientific hucksters to find answers to unassuageable demands for more gadgetry. Clarke's narrator observes:

> Though few realized it as yet, the fall of religion had been paralleled by a decline in science. There were plenty of technologists, but few original workers extending the frontiers of human knowledge. Curiosity remained, and the leisure to indulge in it, but the heart had been taken out of fundamental scientific research. It seemed futile to spend a lifetime searching for secrets that the Overlords had probably uncovered ages before. (p. 75)

The significance of this is not just that scientific method is lost, but that its loss represents a still greater loss: the human yearning to know, to investigate, to long for answers.

Childhood's End means for Clarke, then, the very end of man:

> It was the end of civilization, the end of all that men had striven for since the beginning of time. In the space of a few days, humanity had lost its future, for the heart of any race is destroyed, and its will to survive is utterly broken, when its children are taken from it. (p. 179)

The physical taking of the children, however, is only a symbolic act of a childhood that had been stripped from the people long before.

While Huxley's dystopia is strident in its indictment against Scientism, Clarke's work is more of a mournful elegy for someone or something precious that has died. That something is man's humanity, the childlike which beats in the very fiber of humanity, the daring willingness to wonder. In Walter Miller's *A Canticle for Leibowitz,* this wonder is stripped with finality by the demonic terror of nuclear holocaust.

As do Huxley and Clarke, Walter Miller, Jr. has envisioned in *A Canticle for Leibowitz* a prophetic world. The fascinating variation in this novel is that Miller thrusts the reader ahead in time to a new "Dark Ages," a period after the Flame Deluge in which

> Cities had become puddles of glass, surrounded by vast acreages of broken stone. While nations had vanished from the earth, the lands littered with bodies, both men and cattle and all manner of beasts, together with birds of the air and all things that flew, all things that swam in the rivers, crept in the grass, or burrowed in holes; having sickened and perished, they covered the land, and yet where the demons of the Fallout covered the countryside, the bodies for a time would not decay, except in contact with fertile earth.[25]

In a sense, the novel is a restructuring of history, an archaeological dig on a time not yet happened in order to discover what led to that time. The excavation, however, is finally into the spirit of man:

> "Look at him!" the scholar persisted. "No, but it's too dark now. You can't see the syphilis outbreak on his neck the way the bridge of his nose is being eaten away. Paresis. But he was undoubtedly a moron to begin with. Illiterate, superstitious, murderous. He diseases his children. For a few coins he would kill them. He will sell them anyway, when they are old enough to be useful. Look at him, and tell me if you see the progeny of a once-mighty civilization? What *do* you see?"
>
> "The image of Christ," grated the monsignor, surprised at his own sudden danger. "What did you expect me to see?" (p. 106)

Relentlessly Miller leads us along that parallel path, the human spirit and his fantasized history, to the immediate present where Brother Joshua discovers this: "Destiny always seems decades away, but suddenly it's not decades away; it's right *now.* But maybe destiny is always right now, right here, right this very instant, maybe" (p. 236). The question of *A Canticle for Leibowitz* is whether we can escape the past. Are we doomed to react the tragedy of our historical errors? Can our *now* shape our future? As does Huxley, Miller depicts a world through which he shows us what paths to avoid at all costs.

Surely the dystopian author, like the fantasist, is tremendously relevant to our time. Like fantasy, dystopian literature perceives a grave imbalance. Implicitly, without moralism and didacticism, it suggests a corrective. One essential difference between the two literatures is that of tenor. While the dystopian considers our time with a grave cynicism and grim despair, the fantasist holds stubbornly to a belief in rejuvenation; that man can change, that man can meet the challenges of his age, that man can not merely survive but find at the end of the struggle a sense of joy. This is not to suggest that the fantasist is blithely idealistic, a surreal dreamer properly relegated to his never-never land while we get on with the basic tragedy of life. Indeed, the fantasist shares in common with the dystopian the compelling obligation to engage our reality.

It may be true, as Walter Wangerin Jr., has remarked, that fantasy always deals with the "immeasurable," while science fiction deals with the "measureable."[26] If this is the case, science fiction still clings to realism. Daily life for most persons consists of measurements and quantification—from pouring three scoops of coffee into the pot at a certain morning hour to setting the alarm clock at night. Certainly science fiction dares the unknown, but it seeks to shape and define it into measureable terms by its scientific and technological wizardry. Fantasy is more nearly akin to that theological abstraction of faith, the willing embrace of the numinous, the unknown, the immeasureable, the unquantifiable. As such fantasy finds its proper home in the literary tradition of myth.

Fantasy and Myth

"The present interest in myth," according to Charles Moorman, "reflects a need and search for order and certainty in the midst of the apparent chaos and disorder of the twentieth century."[27] While this interest in myth is large in the present age, as Moorman suggests, the nature and meaning of myth seem to be often misunderstood. The misunderstanding may be due in part to the confusing use of terms. A literary work may be described variously as mythic, mythological, or mythopoeic, and it may be said to contain a mythos.[28] Furthermore, contemporary readers often infer from the term *myth* a sense of incipient falsehood, a deliberate effort to lead astray.

Contrary to the popular conception of myth as a "delightsome lie," Mircea Eliade argues in his study *Myth and Reality* that "In archaic societies and in recent consideration once again, 'myth' means a 'true story' and, beyond that, a story that is a most precious possession because it is sacred, exemplary, significant."[29] Moreover, Eliade adds that myth is "living, in the sense that it supplies models for human behavior and, by that very fact, gives meaning and value to life."[30] It is in this sense that fantasy may be described as myth. Le Guin has frequently described her work as myth and means by it that

> The way of art, after all, is neither to cut adrift from the emotions, the sense, the body, etc., and sail off into the void of pure meaning, nor to blind the mind's eye and wallow in irrational, amoral meaninglessness—but to keep open the tenuous, difficult, essential connections between The two extremes.. To connect. To connect idea with value, sensation.with intuition, cortex with cerebellum.
> The true myth is precisely one of these connections.[31]

So, too, is the true fantasy one of these connections.

I agree with Moorman that there is a longing for myth in our present age. From what conditions does this longing arise? When a civilization becomes highly structured, the need for and presence of myth seem to diminish. Such a society establishes structures of laws as a guide for meaning and action. Increasingly, such structures supplant a vital relationship with divine law with an essentially static system of human law. The compelling benefit of a system of human laws seems to be their immediate apparency. Everyone knows when such a law is broken simply because it is so recorded in some codification of laws. The considered value of such laws often lies in a direct proportion to the rigidity or sureness of them. The more often a law may be questioned, manipulated, or circumvented, the weaker it is. Thus human law seems a sure and immediately accessible structure of determining what behavior is acceptable to society.

On the other hand, myth in fantasy is always more abstract. Myth supplies an ethical imperative flowing from a supranatural authority. It is inscribed on the human spirit rather than code books. Myth provides a dynamic sense of fulfilling a divine will *in* time rather than simply following the rules and regulations *of* a time. Divine law cannot be made into mere system, and indeed it is precisely in defiance of "mere system" that myth exists.

This tension between rule books and a sense of divine will becomes a powerful subplot in Frank Herbert's *Dune Trilogy*. When the vision of Maud'Dib degenerates to mere legalism, the heart of Dune becomes as arid as its desert. The degeneration occurs simultaneously with the huge surge in temple rites, theological hucksters, and drug-induced euphorias in Dune. Compelling meaning becomes only memory while the people prance through their religious regimens. In conversation with his Fremen leader Stilgar, Paul Maud'Dib, the rightful Duke Atreides, states:

> 'We live by the Atreides Law now, Stil. The Fremen Law that the blind should be abandoned in the desert applies only to the blind. I am not blind. I live in the cycle of being where the war of good and evil has its arena. We are at a turning point in the succession of ages and we have our parts to play.[32]

But shortly thereafter Paul Maud'Dib confesses to his beloved concubine, and the mother of his children, Chani:

> 'Ahh, laws,' he said. He crossed to the window, pulled back the draperies as though he could look out. 'What's law? Control? Law filters chaos and what drips through? Serenity? Law—our highest ideal and our basest nature. Don't look too closely at the law. Do, and you'll find the rationalized interpretations, the legal casuistry, which is just another word for death.'[33]

The significance of myth, then, is this. Myth seeks in the midst of changing temporal events one unchanging, authoritative center of meaning. It is opposed to a highly structured society that compiles bodies of laws to govern every aspect of life. The first welcomes change as a chance to express the one authoritative voice in a new way; the other abhors change as either a threat to the status quo or as the onerous burden of compiling new laws. When Moorman observes that there is a new longing for myth in our age, implied is the fact that the age is seeking a clearer, simpler ethical guide than our stacks of legal code books.

On one level, then, myth is displaced as a center for meaning with the growth of centralized political and legal structures. Such is the case in Herbert's *Dune Trilogy*. But a society also becomes more structured as it becomes more technological, and in a sense the growth of western civilization may be traced by the concomitant increase in codification of laws and the increase in technological expertise. The rage for order is accompanied by sure and certain signs that order is reciprocated with some kind of tangible benefit. This technology supplies. Technology is always the fruit of a highly structured society.[34] In his analysis of modern society, *The Abolition of Man,* C.S. Lewis argued convincingly that such advancement always exacts a certain toll upon the spirit of mankind: "There neither is nor can be any simple increase of power on Man's side. Each new power won *by* man is a power *over* man as well. Each advance leaves him weaker as well as stronger. In every victory, besides being the general who triumphs, he is also the prisoner who follows the triumphal car."[35]

Two common social movements, then, contribute to the dislocation of myth. The first is reliance upon political structures to provide readily evident guides for living. The second is the expectation that life can be improved by technological expertise to the point where man has no need for divine benefaction. In the post-Naturalistic era of the twentieth century, man has often found avenues toward human autonomy at best unsatisfactory. Faced with the compelling need to revivify values in an age which professes no need for such values, modern mythmakers attempt to refocus attention upon the ground of spiritual reality. Looking to that groundwork, they say, we can perhaps again refashion the spiritual foundation for life. How does that restructuring take place? To answer this, we must probe the means by which an author uses myth, and the ends to which he uses myth. Particularly revealing of the issue is the seminal work of Mircea Eliade on myth.

While recognizing that "Myth is an extremely complex cultural reality, which can be approached and interpreted from various and complementary viewpoints," Eliade nonetheless constructs a definition for myth that embraces many of these viewpoints. Its very inclusiveness requires that his definition be printed in full:

> Myth narrates a sacred history; it relates an event that took place in a primordial Time, the fabled time of the "beginnings." In other words, myth tells how, through the deeds of Supernatural Beings, a reality came into existence, be it the whole of reality, the Cosmos, or only a fragment of reality.... Myth, then, is always an account of a "creation;" it relates how something was produced, began to *be.* Myth tells only of that which *really* happened, which manifested itself completely.... In short, myths describe the various and sometimes dramatic breakthroughs of the sacred (or the "supernatural") into the World.[36]

Eliade thus establishes the premise that myth recounts some manifestation of divine will, power, and direction in human life.

Since this manifestation is always generative, since it begins things in new direction, this creative act is therefore also determinative upon man. By that I mean simply that the activity guides man in the time following the creative act. By virtue of the creative act, the supernatural power does not finish its activity. Rather, it initiates an activity and a power that abide with man in all the created order. It provides an exemplary pattern, an ethical structure *by virtue of the way the particular order is created.* Thus, I would argue, myth is an accounting of the nature of the universe and particularly a revelation of the sacred presence of divine mandates in the created order.

Myth, then, always attempts to glimpse a divine order which is continually unfolding itself in the created pattern. Myth is continuing story. Eliade argues that "if the World *exists*, it is because Supernatural beings exercised creative powers in the 'beginning.' But after the cosmogony and the creation of man other events occurred, and *man as he is today* is the direct result of those mythical events, he is constituted by those events. He is mortal because something happened *in illo tempore.*"[37] As men participate in the continuing story, one might say, he may exercise his faculties either to read the story truly, or to attempt to rewrite it to accord with his own demands. One learns to read the story truly by seeking the sacred presence of the divine power immanent in life. One attempts to rewrite the story by establishing one's own autonomy through man-made laws and structures which deliberately ignore the divine law. Such a situation is depicted by C.S. Lewis in *That Hideous Strength* in which we find the dialectic between *Logres,* the community governed by divine law and *Britain*, the worldly community which abrogates divine law and supplants it with human automony. We begin to walk the path toward Britain, Lewis would say, as we begin to ignore the myth, the spiritual fabric of life. Not willing to hear, we hear less and less the divine commands which are shouted throughout the universe. All life becomes merely matter. Then the myths are all illusions, fables, or lies.

Should one will to hear, to see, to understand, even the stones would cry out to this divine order. So, then, myth employs story to initiate new hearing, new seeing, new understanding of timeless, divine truths. Modern myth, like the old stories, attempts to glimpse the presence of the sacred in life; the reality of the generation of all creation, and the ongoing, abiding presence of the generative power as it continues to reveal itself in its created order. All myth seeks *beginnings;* but it does so only so that the present order may be known more clearly. By myth the present, and the past event which shaped the present, coalesce. In myth we are at the primordial time, and by seeing *that* time, the true meaning of the story, we are better able to shape the nature of our present time to reveal the will of the creator. Thus, in a sense, *our* time is re-created by looking to the cosmogony of all earthly time. We see it in the light of origins and divine purposes, rather than in terms of our purposes at our time.

When myths point to this spiritual origin through certain regular patterns, these patterns become known as archetypes. The term "archetype" is particularly open to ambiguity, it seems, and is used with a variety of interpretations. Maud Bodkin has provided a useful definition by discussing archetypes as "themes having a particular form or pattern which persists amid variation from age to age, and which corresponds to a pattern or configuration of emotional tendencies in the minds of those who are stirred by the theme."[38] Bearing in mind Bodkin's concept of recurring but varying themes which evoke emotional tendencies in the mind of the reader (or what I have previously called "anagogic insights"), one might also turn to Northrop Frye's distinction between archetype and myth in the glossary to *Anatomy of Criticism.* While Frye's comments on myth are rather narrowly confined within his particular theory, his definition of archetype is helpful by making Bodkin's view specific to literature. For Frye, an archetype is "a symbol, usually an image, which recurs often enough in literature to be recognizable as an element of one's literary experience as a whole."[39] It is a turning inward for answers to man's need, rather than turning outward to the structures afforded by the present age. Le Guin comments:

> The great fantasies, myths, and tales are indeed like dreams: they speak *from* the unconscious *to* the unconscious, in the *language* of the unconscious—symbol and archetype. Though they use words, they work the way music does: they short-circuit verbal reasoning, and go straight to the thoughts that lie too deep to utter. They cannot be translated fully into the language of reason, but only a Logical Positivist, who also finds Beethoven's Ninth Symphony meaningless, would claim that they are therefore meaningless. They are profoundly meaningful, and usable—practical—in terms of ethics; of insight; of growth.[40]

The principal issue is that an archetype is a recurring pattern in literature which points to spiritual themes or experiences common to mankind.[41]

An example of an archetype in mythic literature would be the pattern of birth and rebirth, the idea that by seeking a primitive origin one finds the place of true beginning and thereby is reborn. Often this is symbolized in literature by a descent into a cave or tunnel of the earth. In his discussion of the *regressus ad uteram,* or the birth and rebirth archetype, Eliade remarks that there is always "the initiatory passage through a *vagina dentata,* or the dangerous descent into a cave or assimilated to the mouth or the uterus of Mother Earth. All these adventures are in fact initiatory ordeals, after accomplishing which the victorious hero acquires a new mode of being."[42]

This particular archetype of mythic literature which engages a quest for origins is significant by its extensive use in contemporary fantasy. The instances of a character going "under earth" to emerge reborn are too numerous to list. On a spiritual plane, the archetype suggests a dying to this world in order to regain clear insight of an absolute reality which will give new direction and patterns for growth in the temporal world. By undergoing the mythic rebirth, the individual is radically changed or reborn. One such instance we find, for example, in *The Hobbit* where a terrified Bilbo Baggins stands on the threshold of the cave leading down to the lair of the terrible dragon Smaug. The narrator comments of Bilbo: "Going on from there was the bravest thing he ever did. The tremendous things that happened afterwards were as nothing compared to it. He fought the real battle in the tunnel alone, before he ever saw the vast danger that lay in wait."[42] Going down into "the great bottommost cellar or dungeon-hall of the ancient dwarves right at the Mountain's root" represents also a going down of Bilbo within himself, plumbing the caverns of his own psyche to dredge up whatever he can of courage and self-confidence. Having undergone that spiritual process, he is genuinely transformed.

This I would call the spiritual process. In specifically theological terms we find this particular archetype repeated in all great western religions: the dying and rising corn god, the death of Christ and the descent into hell, and others. The common motif is the sense of dying to this world to be reborn in control of one's world. In a world of rapid change, myth touches upon something enduring and fixed.

We may say, then, that characterizing fantasy is a reliance upon story in the traditional sense of tale-telling. A crowd of modern novelistic techniques is shoving brute shoulders to the forefront of attention: stream of consciousness, the novel of surfaces, topical novels, historical novels, political novels. Fantasy relies upon the age-old tradition of story telling.

Yet, this story is unique from two closely allied genres. Fantasy lacks the rigidity of allegory, and is more open-ended, speculative, and probing than that genre. While closely related to science fiction, fantasy is not dependent for its existence upon certain standard features of that genre.

Most properly, fantasy is a kind of myth, a story which stands in opposition to the iron-clad pragmatism of the age and seeks to return man to a sense of origins and divine significance. It affirms a meaning which is the ground of reality for humankind.

This reality which calls from the distant past, and yet speaks clearly in the present age is what fantasy seeks to head. A technological age depersonalizes people, so that we find in our age not what Martin Buber called the *I* longing for communion with the *Thou*, but rather the *It* standing silently with hands pressed to ears. The hope, the anticipation of fantasy and mythic literature is that by bringing a power larger than man but apparent through man to bear upon this world, we can once again kindle the light of the human spirit. The nature of that power, as we shall see in future chapters, is constituted of enduring and indomitable values such as heroism, chivalry, a sense of good over against evil.

Chapter Three
Character

Story, a "make-believe" tale which nonetheless may bear crushing relevance, lies at the heart of fantasy. If, however, story is to bear relevance, to be applicable to the everyday lives of the readers, to open insight as to how one should then live, these relevances, applications, and insights must arise through characters living the story immediately. Fantasy never attempts to offer the reader a "moral," a nugget of irreducible and apodictic truth which we can carry in a pocket of our mind. Story offers lessons in experience, and those lessons we obtain by the experiences of the characters. Fantasy has thereby developed special kinds of characters.

Several traits of these characters may be observed briefly; others deserve larger consideration. In the former group we find traits such as commonness, naivete, and animal characters. In the latter group we find the more complex literary patterns of the childlike and heroism. These will be examined in the following three divisions.

Commonness of Character

The characters of fantasy are largely people or beings of a common nature. They might be any one of us in the tale—and that is precisely the point. We are not asked to stand on the outside and survey this tale from detached perspective; we are asked to enter into it so that the story becomes ours. Thus we find characters quite like us. Granted, they may not always be human characters, but they are like us. Tolkien's hobbit far prefers an easy chair and a good pipe full of tobacco to an adventure. Elwin Ransom of Lewis's *Space Trilogy* is a philologist by profession. In *Watership Down* the main characters are some raggedy, ignoble hares. Many of the central characters of fantasy are country people. The wizard Ged of Le Guin's *Earthsea Trilogy* is the son of a bronzesmith on a rustic island, and is himself referred to as "goatherd." Many Welsh fantasies, such as Evangeline Walton's

Mabinogion tales, have central characters who are country folk.

I remark that by virtue of the common character it is thereby easier for the reader to enter into the story, to see himself in the action. Even though we may all like to play Superman, in literature we always seem to stand outside the larger than life hero. He is ably equipped, after all, to fight his own battles. In fact, we usually know at the outset who will win; we're just not certain how. Thus the pattern of the detective and western genres. But with the common character we recognize the shortcomings (they are our own), and want to join in and help. When he gets knocked down, which occurs frequently, we would like to help from the safety of our easy chair. Maybe between the both of us we can pull it off. If the first reason for the common character, then, is ready identification of the reader with the character, a second is the value of this character's naivete.

The common character is naive; that is, he retains a certain innocence and he is disinterested in terms of worldly allegiances. The common character is naive in the sense of not having become cynical, hard-bitten, or spoiled by the world about him. He retains the child-like trait of wonder, the willingness to engage adventure. Often the characters of fantasy are children, although this is certainly not a prerequisite for the genre. I think it is only because the authors see in children the willingness to wonder which we adults so often lose. This subject will be examined more extensively in our consideration of the childlike.

Several qualifications, however, should be made here. First the characters are common, but they are what literary criticism would call "well-rounded" or whole characters. Herein lies another distinction from allegory, for in allegory the reader finds characters *representing* something, and thereby often failing to find human wholeness. The characters are stereotypical in their signaling of an abstraction such as Lust, Virtue, Rationalism, and so forth. The characters pass in quick review. There are often many such characters for when their allegorical function is fulfilled they are left behind. Such disposable characters we find, for example, in David Lindsay's *Voyage to Arcturus,* a work of large influence but more clearly allegory than fantasy. Moreover, it is bad allegory, for the consistency of the stereotypes to an allegorical plane is flawed. It is nearly impossible to discern a logical order to the characters; they are so vaporous and transient. They are merely steppingstones on Maskull's journey.

Further light on this distinction between allegory and

fantasy characters may be shed by C. S. Lewis's *The Pilgrim's Regress*. Here Lewis did in fact craft a very successful allegory. Not only are the stock characters clearly discernible, but Lewis took pains in the chapter headnotes to remind us of what the characters clearly mean. The work is a marvellous piece of allegory; a sizzling scholarly roast of 20th century pretensions, age-old human errors, and enduring spiritual perversions. Why then was Lewis disappointed with the work to the degree that in a later Preface to it and in several letters he publicly denigrated the work? His own response in the Preface to the Third Edition cites "needless obscurity, and an uncharitable temper."[1] But, as Lewis considers the issue further in the Preface, it becomes evident that for him allegory lacked the sense of mystery, of exploration, of real human life that he had by that time located in fantasy.

In sum, we would say, then, that the point of fantasy is not to provide tidy morals, but to provide growth by experience. In fantasy we learn not morals but lessons on life's way. It is necessary, therefore, that the reader clearly recognizes this in the characters of the story. The characters may be called to be heroes, but first of all to be human; to recognize the human situation for what it is, and what possibly can be done about it.

This does not always mean that the characters are in fact human, for fantasy often provides animals or mythical beasts as central characters. Sometimes such characters are gifted with reason and speech, but this is coincidental to the demands of the story. In Robert Siegel's *Alpha Centauri* the story itself is about centaurs trying to locate their true home. The child Becky who enters into their world is the foreigner. Similarly, Richard Adams' fantasies focus exclusively upon animals. In each instance, however, the animal characters are threatened by something associated with power, technology, or scientific advancement; in short, they are threatened by man's rage for achievement. This is a rage which uses animals, plants, rivers, air, as things. The animals, on the other hand, are struggling for a simplicity and reverence for life—and also simply to survive.

The literary origins of the animal figures lie in the fairy tale and the beast fable. In the fairy tale, however, animal figures are often ambivalent. On one page a big bad wolf lurks with a lecherous heart for the lovely Red Riding Hood. On the next page three pigs bounce from travel to travail only to endure by the hairs on their stubby chins. Usually fairy tale animals pose a threat to human life, particularly in the early, often violent tales collected by the Brothers Grimm. We have bowdlerized many of these tales for modern juveniles, but it remains a fact that few if any animals in fairy tales work in consistent value systems approaching humankind.[2]

Animal figures in modern fantasy are more akin to those of the beast fable—and the lineage of fantasy is always to the Middle Ages, the Romance, and its allied literatures. Evidence of this is the appearance of Walter Wangerin's enormously popular *The Book of the Dun Cow*, a modern fantasy beast fable that picks up precisely where Chaucer and Henryson left off, in an exciting rendition of that vainglorious cock Chauntecleer who better than any man, perhaps, tutors us in human frailty. The beast fable shares this in common with fantasy: the characters are common, and they are struggling with matters of the human spirit, for these characters are of course anthropomorphized. Charles Muscatine, commenting on Chaucer's "Nun's Priest's Tale," observes that "Fable respects the boundary between animal fictions and the human truth it illustrates. But the whole spirit of this poem is to erase or at least overleap the boundaries...."[3]

There are marked differences in the use to which authors put the beast fable. It lends itself nicely to allegory, and Henryson, for one, plays the game for all it's worth. Henryson is concerned with the *moralitas* in his "Morall Fabillis" and points it steadily toward the road of Christian redemption. His fable is garbed in black with a high white collar. Chaucer can be as metaphysical as anyone, but finally his work bears the mark of realism and human sympathy. In his tale there is a bit of the clergy's collar, a bit of the philosopher's cape, the pilgrim's hood, the hack's worn britches. Chaucer, in short, explores the human condition. The success of Walter Wangerin, Jr., a Lutheran minister who studied for a time in medieval literatures, lies in his complete transmogrification of the old fable into modern fantasy. Although a discussion of the work anticipates future discussion in this study, it is illuminating of the nature of the beast fable in modern fantasy.

Among the traits which characterize fantasy literature, as we shall see, the most important and also the most difficult to handle artistically is the struggle between good and evil. The danger on the one hand is that evil is represented simply by strange characters—dragons and ogres—who are readily identifiable as villains. By such easy identification, evil comes in too familiar a guise and loses its hideousness. On the other hand, the danger is that evil predominates so hideously that good isn't given much of a chance. On the third hand, as a character of this novel would say, the struggle itself may be such an insipid affair that the reader doesn't care who wins. With some of the Pentagonian complexities of modern fantasy, in which one seems cursed to sit in on a meeting of joint chiefs of staff, one feels they all deserve to lose.

The alternative, and what good fantasy must achieve, is an evil that is formidable, a hero who though subject to all manner of weakness manages to persevere over evil, and a struggle between the two worth engaging.

In *The Book of the Dun Cow* Wangerin has given us an evil that is not only frightening but downright fearful.[4] Cockatrice and his brood of vipers (thousands of them by a progenitive ingenuity seldom seen in literature) are a malignant force in the world that threatens the kingdom of Chaunticleer, and with it the hope of all kingdoms. This is not an evil to be sought out on a lonely quest or one which looms as a remote possibility; rather it is a terrifying presence, one impossible to avoid.

Chaunticleer, the magnificent rooster and ruler of the land, is not one to evade the task. The book closes in a monumental battle. Yet, the real joy, the sheer pleasure of the book, lies in the subtle but sure movement of the plot and the role each character plays in its resolution. Wangerin never loses control of the strange personalities that people this world, nor does he lose sight of their destiny in the climax of the story.

In this world we meet a marvel of beasts. Mundo Cani Dog, a shuffling, sniffling, sorrowful carriage of bones and protuberant nose, achieves a heroism beyond expection—surely beyond the expectation of Chaunticleer, who berates him in such terms as "rug" and "satchel." John Wesley Weasel is another marvelous creation, whose vigorous spirit and volatile speech provide constant amusement and action. Pertelot, with the crimson neck and white feathers, is as exquisite and compassionate a beauty as one could hope for in literature. And Chaunticleer himself—here is the *nonpareil* who as such is invested with bits and pieces of everyman, a rooster who undergoes a conversion akin to Saint Paul's, who thunders Lauds with such awesome force that the forest shakes, who can deliver a tent revival sermon that leaves the animals shouting "AMEN!," who struts with pride and yet in the grief to which he falls echoes the words of King David lamenting the death of Absalom.

A host of common creatures in this uncommon world people a middle ground—the victims, for good or bad, of the struggle. Here we find hens ranging from malapert sauciness to thoroughly domesticated docility. Gloriously stupid turkeys greet each change of fortune with a blind stoicism. We find Ebenezer Rat, who is bad but not evil and whose greedy activities prefigure the coming of Cockatrice.

And there are the others from what Chaim Potok calls in *Asher Lev* "the other side," that dark and terrible domain of evil. Cockatrice, the abomination sent from below by Wyrm to destroy the land forever, and Wyrm himself, who rends the earth in a gaping chasm of death, are the primary manifestations. Wangerin provides an accretion of evil; each revelation more powerful and hideous than the last. Evil, once welcomed in the world, consumes the world. Like Chaunticleer, the reader feels compelled to cry out: "You gave me hope! O my God, you taught me to *hope*! And then you killed me." The resolution of the struggle with the appearance of the Dun Cow comes with surprise and power simply because these beasts have placed us entirely within the purview of evil's domain.

In its purest literary lineage, the beast fable stands midway between allegory and modern fantasy. In the origins of the form the fable characters represent certain abstractions, but they retain the homeliness and realism which at once makes them more human than the figures of allegory. In the modern tradition, fantasy has frequently used animal characters to insure a kind of earthiness and commonality of its characters. Frequently, human characters in fantasy have animal friends who are gifted with voice, who are guides to action, who are a solace in a troubled world and a companion in loneliness. For example, Ged from Le Guin's *Earthsea Trilogy* is always accompanied by his Otak and Yarrow has her harrekki. Whether as companions or central characters, however, fantasy literature maintains from the beast fable a menagerie of animals. Without variation, whether the animal is a centaur, unicorn, hross, otak, dragon, or common dog, the animal characters familiarize and locate the story in the common storehouse of human experience.

The Childlike

I have mentioned that the common characters of fantasy are often naive. That term is markedly pejorative in modern vernacular. The naive person is a dunce, an incompetent.

"Sophisticated" people are the survivors if not winners. They also usually don't like fantasy. But naivete in fantasy is always a good thing which suggests that the character has retained a willingness to wonder, has not been despoiled by the world's affairs, has not been made hard-bitten and cynical of life. And these latter characters, the pragmatists, the despoiled, the hard-bitten and cynical are often the villains of fantasy.

It would also be villainous, however, to simply remark that fantasy works often have children as protagonists, therefore children as characters are a trait of the genre. Not only would this be critical villainy but, worse, it would be bad logic. The task is to determine why there are many children as protagonists by determining the nature of the childlike. If we can determine this, we have a sense of a *human* character trait of which adult characters in fantasy may also partake. To provide a literary framework, consider first the evolution of the childlike from the seething waters of Romanticism, and then specifically through the clearing stream of Charles Dickens.

The English appreciation for children is a phenomenon refined in the fires of 19th century industrialization. In the early days of that century, before the factory boilers blasted around the clock and children trooped in for twelve hour shifts, six days a week, to feed those boilers, William Wordsworth claimed in "The Tables Turned" that the child is the father of the man. A bitter tutor the child was to be, but for the time being here was the symbol of a new movement: the child—pure, untainted by demands of science and technology, often possessing a kind of wisdom which sees intuitively the right and wrong of things, and almost always filled with the wonder so cherished by the romantic. The child became a guide to truth and meaning, and the child therefore romps joyfully through many romantic poems. Wordsworth may be forgiven, perhaps. The children of Windemere were quite unlike those grimy, vicious young faces that Charles Dickens found prowling the streets of London.

Dickens wrote of childhood fancy against the background of an already rich tradition. Blake, for example, detailed his intricate vision of the childlike nature which persists into adulthood, and the adulthood incipient in the child. The full title of Blake's Innocence and Experience poems is this: "Songs of Innocence and Experience: Shewing the Two Contrary States of the Human Soul." Man is a composite of a childlike desire to trust and an adult fear of having trust defiled. Blake sings in his introductory song:

> And I made a rural pen,
> And I stained the water clear,
> And I wrote my happy songs,
> Every child may joy to hear.

Even in this happy song there must be made room for the tyger burning bright in the night. God who made the little lamb, and God who "becomes a man of woe/He doth feel the sorrow too," is also the God who made the night, who allows woe.

There is a larger dimension to the childlike vision operating in Blake. Rationalism demanded that everything be submitted to the scrutiny of pure reason. There is little room in Rationalist logic for childlike naivete, and less room for a God who sends both joy and woe. Innocence runs contrary to Rationalism which sought to subject all things to the light of pure reason. Innocence subjects experience to the light of instinct. Harold Bloom defines innocence in Blake as "that state of the human soul in which we ascertain truth as immediate knowledge, for the knower and the known share an unsought natural harmony."[5] The child represents an antithesis to method and process in his spontaneous ability to intuit what is true or false.

Perhaps the most complete analysis of childlike vision in Romanticism was developed by Friedrich Schiller in *Naive and Sentimental Poetry*. In this study Schiller brings together the antithesis of childlike instinct to Rationalism which enamored Blake with the concept of the child as potentiality. Schiller defines the *naive poet* as one characterized by spontaneity, immediacy, and an absence of self-consciousness. The *sentimental poet's* feelings undergo the scrutiny of intellect. His feelings are not free and expressive, but are always put to the test of rational validation and the test of propriety in a larger rational framework of life. The naive poet is in harmony with nature—he taps the well-springs of life with immediacy—while the sentimental poet *seeks* nature, as Schiller says, "precisely because it is lacking in himself." The importance of this being within nature or seeking nature lies in the fact that natural forms, of which the child is a symbol for Schiller, contain what we might be and what we were once: "*They are what we were;* they are *what we should once again become....* They are, therefore, not only the representation of our lost childhood, which eternally remains most dear to us, but fill us with a certain melancholy. But they are also representatives of our highest fulfillment in the ideal, thus evoking in us a sublime tenderness."[6]

Schiller argues that inherent in mankind is a poetic spirit which drives us with a longing for the natural. When the poetic spirit becomes displaced by Rationalism, and when experienced emotions become merely abstractions, man has to seek natural forms rather than enjoying them directly. But the child enjoys this poetic spirit directly, hence "We are touched not because we look down upon the child from the strength of our height and perfection, but rather because we *look upward* from the limitation of our condition...."[7]

This sense has not been lost in modern fantasy. Le Guin comments of fantasy authors that;

> They believe that maturity is not an outgrowing, but a growing up; that an adult is not a dead child, but a child who survived. They believe that all the best faculties of a mature human being exist in the child, and that if these faculties are encouraged in youth they will act well and wisely in the adult, but if they are repressed and denied in the child they will stunt and cripple the adult personality.[8]

Her voice, we shall see, is only part of a larger chorus.

The child not only represents potential, spontaneity, and trust for Charles Dickens, but as with Schiller, the child also represents the cleavages in man's nature. Dickens' art is also the history of what man has lost. Yet Dickens believed, more strongly yet than Schiller perhaps, that it is possible, if not to recapture the past, then to redeem the present. He longed for the childlike naivete which heals, which fills the fractures in life with love and kindness. The spirit of compassion is the spirit which the child brings. In Dickens' depiction, the child moves among men as an outcast, yet touches individual lives with transforming power.

Dickens' novels are filled with lost and lonely children, wandering in the darkest alleys of the human condition, seeking desperately the light of love and friendship. Children became the heroes of Dickens' novels, and he did much to place the child as a literary type for the ensuing century. Dickens' children, I find, share several particular traits.

First, an innate ability to see through sham. Dickens' adult world is filled with masqueraders, people trying to fool others and themselves by being something which they are not. The child intuitively sees through the disguise. He senses what is good and evil with a capacity which does not have to analyze good and evil into categories but instead makes instinctive, intuitive judgments about them.

Second, the child has the ability to maintain purity and innocence. He is of course *corruptible* in Dickens' novels, but he nonetheless maintains an innate sense of the good and will seek the good when allowed to.

Third, the child maintains his imaginative ability. This is perhaps the most important trait for our purposes. The adult world is run by fact and process. Dickens' adults engage in a brutal ritual which they come to call life. In the revealing chapter "Murdering the Innocence" of *Hard Times,* Dickens depicts a systematic teacher trying to convince his charges that a horse is not a free animal who wanders about grassy plains on a hillside or in the imagination, but a gramnivorous quadruped, possessed of so many teeth and such and such characteristics. Somehow, in Dickens' world, the child retains the ability to imagine the horse as a lovely animal, wild and free. For example, in *David Copperfield*, the young David is punished by his stepfather, Murdstone. While imprisoned in his room for hours on end, David's only consolation consists of a small stack of novels left behind by his natural father. David manages to preserve his sense of imaginative freedom by projecting his present circumstances into the fantasy world of those novels. The fantasy liberates and sustains him.

Finally, the child seeks freedom. Dickens' harshest indictment of modern man is that he has constructed mental prisons for himself. He becomes locked into a system from which he cannot escape. The system may be a private world such as greed or vice, or it may be a public function such as that of the minister Chadband who hides behind his clerical facade and refuses to engage life. This locking up of the self is, in Dickens' thought, the most deadly disease. Its symptoms are a withering of love and a failure to help others in need. In short, such imprisonment prevents one from loving others and himself. The child, in Dickens' view, naturally reaches out to others, and seeks the fulfillment of love.

A special emphasis should be given to Dickens' indictment of institutions, for these were, in his estimation, the gravest threat to fantasy and the imagination. Most destructive of these institutions was education, for it held the promise of children in its hands and ground the promise to dust by channeling its subjects into a theoretical framework instead of freeing the childrens' imagination and promise. Dickens launched his most devastating assault upon Master Gradgrind's school in *Hard Times*. It was indeed a hard time for the children of Gradgrind's regime, forced to digest and regurgitate facts by rote, until their very personalities and being were absorbed by the process. Children, for Gradgrind, were "little pitchers before him, who were to be filled with so many facts." The bane of Gradgrind's system is fancy, which has no role in the sterile world of facts. With his philosophy of "Murdering the Innocents," or murdering the innocence of childhood fancy, Gradgrind is enraged when he finds his own children glued to the peephole watching the circus. This human, imaginative dimension of childhood is held in utter contempt.

Dickens waged his attack on such education throughout his major works. In *Bleak House* we discover that much of Richard's chronic indecision is traceable to a faulty education in which he learned "to make Latin Verses of several sorts, in the most admirable manner. But I never heard that it had been anybody's business to find out what his natural bent was, or where his failings lay, or to adapt any kind of knowledge to *him*."[9] This same demand for facts forms the pedagogical premise of Blimber's school in *Dombey and Son*. Dr. Blimber possesses vast resources of facts which he delivers in "such a determined, unimpassioned, inflexible, cold-blooded way." His sister Miss Blimber functions best in the dead languages. "None of your live languages for Miss Blimber. They must be dead—stone dead— and then Miss Blimber dug them up like a ghoul."[10] As with Gradgrind, the primary purpose of this school seems to be the stifling of fancy and any show of passion in the rote assimilation of facts.

There is a fascinating educator and education in *Little Dorrit*. When the Old Father of the Marshalsea receives an inheritance, he adopts a whole new ethical standard to match his wealth. The humble love the Dorrits shared in prison as social outcasts is transformed overnight into a struggle for all the pretenses of social position. These pretenses include refinement in the intellectual graces and necessitate the hiring of Mrs. General as a tutor in those graces. Mrs. General fits well into the Gradgrind system with the added embellishment of being the high priestess of "Prunes and Prisms," the elocutionary passwords to social refinement. Her way of forming a mind, we are told, is to prevent it from forming opinions. Stifle originality at all costs. "Passion," writes Dickens, "was to go to sleep in the presence of Mrs. General, and blood was to change to milk and water." Any little cracks in her vision of reality are healed by the varnish of social pretense. Upper crust fed a hungering mind. In Mrs. General's world and life view, young Amy Dorrit is a hopeless ne'er-do-well, someone who insists on clinging to the small passions of her past, one who dares show emotion. Amy is the outsider in the starched world of social grace.

In *David Copperfield* Dickens presents one of his strongest confrontations between a passionate quest for life and those forces that deny life. Typifying the conflict is David's education under Creakle at Salem House. Creakle, with his inordinate fondness for beating chubby little boys, runs his school with a firmness that devastated any romantic fancy. For David, the incipient novelist, fancy was forced to go underground and he entertained his fellow inmates in the after-hours darkness with tales he had read while a prisoner of the Murdstones.

These educational regimes thrive on "firmness," molding and channeling young minds into a planned system. Creakle, Gradgrind, Blimber, Mrs. General, all exercise their doctrines with unwavering firmness. Anyone under their tutelage who exercises the inklings of fancy and is caught *in flagrante delicto* is visited quickly with wrath and punishment. This firmness, this inability to accept and adapt to the thoughts and dreams of others, presents a constant threat to young David Copperfield's imaginative and exploring mind. One key question in the novel is whether David will survive as a person when denied the opportunity to explore his own individuality, or whether he will discover some inner resource to overcome the firm dictates of others. David's step-father Mr. Murdstone lives by a creed of controlling passion, abjuring David's mother to "control yourself, always control yourself!" Miss Murdstone shares her brother's arid outlook on life, and Dickens at one point condemns her creed of firmness as "diabolical."

Childhood, then, was the first and last gasp of Romanticism as it staggered heavy and uncertain into the adult realization of a mechanical universal order, of a technocratic world ruled by processes that one comes to know too well. As Thomas Hardy grimly attested: "All around you there seemed to be something glaring, garish, rattling, and the noises and glares hit upon the little cell called your life, and shook it, and warped it."[11] For

Hardy, growing up was a process of stripping yourself of wonder, and putting on heavier garb to protect yourself against the cold of the world. The lament of Hardy is that wonder and innocence are irrevocably lost. Dickens wanted us not to believe this. Modern fantasy demonstrates that it is not so.

Modern fantasy often seems to echo Dickens in regard to the child-like and the threat to it by a systematic, institutionalized world. In Madeleine L'Engle's *A Wrinkle in Time* we find a scene typical of fantasy, children enrolled in a Gradgrind-like school and longing for another world. " 'School,'" reflects Meg, "School was all wrong."[12] In *Alpha Centauri,* Robert Siegel provides the same conflict. When Becky's father invites her on the trip that leads to her fantasy adventure, "The principal of her junior high had agreed—reluctantly, since he feared her math would suffer. Becky was overjoyed, for she hated math as much as she loved to read."[13] Similarly, in Susan Cooper's series of *Gray King* books, each fantasy adventure is ushered in by the advent of holidays. It is true, of course, that many fantasies simply evoke another world clean and whole with no allusion to earth-bound trappings such as schools. But it remains a solid motif in fantasy.

No one, perhaps, has used it as extensively and deliberately as C.S. Lewis, who was equally at home in the lecture hall of academe or in fantasy stories. While the former were for students in ivied halls, the latter were often directed to children longing for escape from the classroom.

There are several key reasons why Lewis ostensibly directed his art toward children, or more properly "the childlike." With a subtitle such as "A Story for Children," Lewis reminds us, as does Le Guin, that we are not children, then adults, then middle-aged, then elderly. We are human, and these stages of being form that composite whole of our human nature. We do not graduate at a certain stage from childlikeness. Rather childlikeness remains a part of our nature. Lewis commented in his essay "On Stories" that:

It is usual to speak in a playfully apologetic tone about one's adult enjoyment of what are called 'children's books.' I think the convention a silly one. No book is really worth reading at the age of ten which is not equally (and often far more) worth reading at the age of fifty—except, of course, books of information. The only imaginative works we ought to grow out of are those which it would have been better not to have read at all.[14]

Carl Jung argued similarly in *The Development of Personality* that: "I suspect our contemporary pedagogical and psychological enthusiasm for the child of dishonorable intentions: we talk about the child, but we should mean the child in the adult. For in every adult there lurks a child, something that is always becoming, is never completed, and calls for unceasing care, attention, and education."[15]

In Lewis's view, fantasy recalls childlike wonder into our real, grown-up world, and we gain immeasurably by that recollection:

> But who in his senses would not keep, if he could, that tireless curiosity, that intensity of imagination, that facility of suspending disbelief, that unspoiled appetite, that readiness to wonder, to pity, and to admire? The process of growing up is to be valued for what we gain, not for what we lose. Not to acquire a taste for the realistic is childish in the bad sense; to have lost the taste for marvels and adventures is no more a matter for congratulation than losing our teeth, our hair, our palate, and finally, our hopes.[16]

Many have considered fantasy as unworthy because they presume it to be deceptive, illusory, and therefore false. I have already discussed the fact that fantasy is a means of revealing truth, rather than a means of deceiving. As did Dickens, Lewis pays significant attention to the child's ability to see through sham, to intuitively distinguish between false and true. He asks us not to rationally scrutinize the validity of insights garnered from story; this may come later. First one must intuitively experience the insights. The child, for Lewis, has the intuitive ability to see through the sham of evil and recognize the good. In *The Magician's Nephew* young Digory Kirke quickly sees through the evil designs of his Uncle Andrew. Andrew attempts to explain away his actions: "No, Digory. Men like me who possess hidden wisdom, are freed from common rules just as we are cut off from common pleasures. Ours, my boy, is a high and lonely destiny."[17] To which Digory responds: " 'All it means,' he said to himself, 'is that he thinks he can do anything he likes to get anything he wants.' "

But, like Dickens, Lewis believed children are corruptible. What spoils their imagination, tarnishes their sense of wonder, obscures their ability to distinguish true from false, is in part the spiritually numbing ritual of modern education which attempts to force all of life into process and system. The spirit withers under the reign of facts. Lewis lamented the "Abolition of Man," arguing that we have become men without spirit. We have lost our courage; we no longer dare wonder. This theme threads its way throughout the *Chronicles*. In each tale the children on earth are groaning under regimented education, and it is not until they are freed into the daring wonder of Narnia that they begin to learn. The theme of "Holidays" also prevails throughout the series and culminates in the closing paragraphs of *The Last Battle* in which Aslan proclaims: "The term is over: the holidays have begun. The dream is ended: this is the morning." The guiding purpose of the *Chronicles* is to give holiday to the human imagination—a respite from daily life in order to deal with daily life in new spirit and vigor.

In every *Chronicle* in which earthly children appear, Lewis jibes at educational process. In *The Lion, the Witch and the Wardrobe* Professor Kirke wonders what do they teach them in school. What they teach them is facts but not logic. What they teach them is system but not wonder. Basic assumptions are never defined, nor ever challenged. One has no opportunity to ask—but what does it mean? Lewis considered this enervating to mankind, weakening him, hollowing him out. In *The Voyage of the "Dawn Treader"* Eustace Scrubb is educated to like grain elevators, import and export, and making a profit. Knowing nothing about dragons, it is small wonder that he turns into one. Eustace Scrubb is initially portrayed as the suburban brat, incorrigibly loud-mouthed and also a sissy. This is what such education produces in Lewis's view.

In Narnia he replaces it with the chivalric code of courtesy. When we first meet Peter in his role as High King, he is perhaps the meekest of children, yet in Narnia he is also the most courageous. Here the meek do inherit the earth. Meekness, however, should never be mistaken for servility or cowardice— rather it is the recognition of an authority in one's life and the order that stems from this authority.

Peter has respect for even the lowest of creatures for he sees them as creatures of Aslan and not as natural properties to be used in technological consumption. For Narnia, the medieval scholar Lewis resurrects the code of chivalry as a standard for behavior. One might recall Chaucer's description of the "verray parfit, gentil knyght" of the *Canterbury Tales*. Here the courteous knight abides by the chivalric code of "Trouthe and honour, fredom and curteisie," or loyalty, honorable deeds, nobility, and courtly manner. Chaucer's knight is described as thoroughly courageous, but always mild and meek in deportment. Such a life style can only come from service to a powerful and absolute sovereign.

This concept of service qualifies the theme of "Holidays" for Lewis. There is order in Lewis's concept of learning. According to this code education is not doing anything you like. Education must be pointed toward enduring values and toward absolute meanings. Such education has a guide not in the world of fact, but in the world of the spirit, the world attained by the imagination.

We see in much modern fantasy, then, the use of childlike characters emerging from a deliberate literary tradition. The values of that tradition remain the same for modern fantasy. It holds that the childlike imagination, although easily damaged or perverted, is a thing of infinite worth. It is through wonder that we cross the threshold of another world. It is through faith and compassion that we dare bring the lessons of this other world to bear upon our own. And that is the heroic task of fantasy literature.

Heroism

By placing large emphasis upon the commonplace nature of fantasy protagonists, I do not intend that they are incapable of heroic actions. Indeed the former emphasis is absolutely necessary to understand heroism in fantasy. Heroism in the modern age has been obfuscated by popularity. We have instead of the hero—the superstar. The glittering idol of media and fans, the superhype of the popular arena, could not be further from the true nature of the literary hero.

To understand the fantasy hero properly though—for this common character does achieve great and noble deeds—it is also necessary to locate this hero in the larger literary tradition. Certain traits of the literary hero have remained fairly standard in the shift of time. For example, in classical literature the hero was distinguished first by his uncertain paternity. Consider the case of Oedipus. The obscurity of his lineage is of course the subject matter of the Oedipus cycle of plays. The significance of such obscurity, however, rests in the hero's superhuman powers. Since he possesses intelligence or physical powers seemingly beyond the grasp of common man, the hero is considered partly divine. His obscure lineage leaves open this possibility: that the gods have invested superhuman capabilities in this mortal.

The task of this hero was twofold: to defeat some threat to the people and to lead the people into his perception of order. Thus the hero's deeds are for the people and for the purpose of establishing order free from internal or external threat. The classical hero acts for all mankind. Thomas Greene observes that "The Act which induces heroic awe must be performed by a single individual or at most by a very small group of individuals. The hero must be acting for the community, the City; he may incarnate the city, but he must be nonetheless an individual with a name."[18] In *Oedipus Rex,* for example, we find the hero in precisely this position. Once before Oedipus delivered the people by answering the riddle of the Sphinx and breaking the drought upon the land. At the beginning of this play we find the people again scattered before the door of Oedipus beseeching his favor. The hero never secludes himself from his people, but as in this play comes before them to answer their supplication. The deeds of the hero are for the people.

Through much of literary history this pattern for heroism was little changed. The hero, because of supernatural gifts, can act for others in such a way as to restore order in their lives. During the great flowering of heroic literature in the middle ages, when eyes and hearts turned toward the lordly king and the shining blade of the knight, western literary heroism achieved a kind of pinnacle. Above all stands Arthur, the king of uncertain lineage. Was he Uther's son? A bastard? A gift from fire and wave as Merlin reports? A god in human form? Arthur's heroism resides in his incarnation of the divine order in the affairs of men. His powerful *comitatus* of knights was the effective force of his heroic vision.

The fantasy hero lies in this tradition; but with a difference. First of all, as common character he is all too well aware of his frightful mortality. He knows he is not a god. The deeds to which he is called are engaged with mortal fear and trembling. Second, he is often lonely, terribly lonely, for his deeds are often engaged far from the idol-worshipping throng; sometimes in an altogether different world. Yet it is often for this unacknowledging crowd that he acts. The heart of modern fantasy is this premise: that a very ordinary character is tested beyond expectation or human hope for success. He cannot run to the organized assistance that our world offers. Ultimately he must rely on nothing more than human imagination and intelligence. The wonder of fantasy is thus what *we might do;* not what others do for us. In his discussion of Le Guin's *Earthsea Trilogy,* George Slusser comments of the protagonist that "Ged is an idealized hero...and an everyman. His powers seem exceptional, and yet he wins great battles with the means we all possess."[19] That is the surprise fantasy holds for us. Third, fantasy heroism often requires a test of strength and endurance. One expects Lancelot to win in Arthur's jousts. As Tennyson reports in his telling of the legend in *Idylls of the King,* "they fall before his name." The fantasy hero has no such status about him. He always walks on the slippery edge of fear and failure. His heroism is established at considerable risk, and always with some wit and cunning that more than make up for his physical frailty.

Having said this, one affirms that fantasy is filled with thrilling and dangerous deeds. The common character is not insipid. He is merely mortal. But as mortal, he is free in a way that the classical hero never could be. Manlove has pointed out that "Any conception of a hero demands that the hero's actions be substantially based on free choice and human will."[20] The fact that the common character freely chooses terrible risk ennobles his heroism.

In an age that celebrates the "anti-hero," there seems to be some residual longing in the heart of man for those great and noble deeds. Byron's lament in Canto I of *Don Juan,*

> I want a hero: an uncommon want,
>   When every year and month sends forth a new one,
> Till, after cloying the gazettes with cant,
>   The age discovers he is not the true one,

may typify the modern thirst for heroism. But to this thirst is served up a steady diet of unsatisfying idols. They serve only to exacerbate the longing. With the advent of the anti-hero, some have proclaimed the longing simply fruitless. It was Nietzsche, perhaps, who with his Overman gave birth to the twentieth-century anti-hero, the man left with nothing to value, not even his own being. The narrator of Dostoevsky's *Notes from Underground* claims that the modern hero is the man with the capacity to utterly defile himself. We have in twentieth-century literature, insisted an Oedipus or an Arthur, Camus's Meursault who finds even his murder trial so utterly futile that "I felt like vomiting, and I had only one idea: to get it over, to go back to my cell, and sleep...and sleep."

The anti-hero resides in a prison of inaction. Worse, he doesn't care about it. Victor Brombert makes a telling comment

about Jean-Paul Sartre's "Intellectual Hero" that typifies much
of the modern anti-heroic sensibility:

> Thrown back within his own limits, Sartre's intellectual knows
> the full insipidity of his existence. For *existence,* he discovers,
> is precisely this: to be one's own taste, to drink oneself without
> thirst. He feels walled in, surrounded, isolated and rejected. *Le
> Mur, La Chambre, Intimite, Huis-Clos*—so many of Sartre's
> titles betray metaphorically the feeling of alienation within a
> prison, an exile within oneself.[21]

This prison of the individual intelligence also has no exit, for
"The more sharply he perceives the clash between his view of
himself and the mirror-perspective of others, the more
inescapably he locks himself up in his own consciousness, living
out his 'latent solitude' to the point of impossibility."[21] In *The
Waste Land*, T.S. Eliot sounds the echo of this isolated
consciousness:

> I have heard the key
> Turn in the door once and turn once only
> We think of the key, each in his prison
> Thinking of the key, each confirms the prison.

It is this intellectual prison of one's own mind, commonly
accepted as unavoidable, that modern fantasy seeks to liberate.

The quest here is one which seeks a center of value and
meaning in life and art which provides genuine satisfaction to
human longing, which arises from within the human spirit to
replenish that same spirit, and which ultimately directs a vision
outward from that spirit to include all humanity in the discovery
of value and meaning. In an age which readily claims to be bereft
of any normative, traditional guide to value, the task demands a
spirit of new heroism, and a uniquely human one. This heroic task
is not the classical one to destroy a presence threatening the
normative value of the age, but rather it was one to construct
some order and meaning out of the remnants of a self-destructive
age. The task, then, is twofold: discovery of a locus of value in the
heroic character, and revivification of value in others by heroic
actions.

The struggle of the hero to make of himself a repository of
value, a discoverer of self-worth, proves a formidable affair.
Translating this discovery into terms which revivify value in
others proves entirely as formidable. The heroic quest is always a

frightening quest and few are willing to undertake it. The curious quality of fantasy literature is its assiduous belief that even the most common character can and indeed must undertake it.

As I remarked earlier, sometimes the common character is called to a wholly other world to perform his deeds. This emphasizes the loneliness and individuality of his quest. But even though enacted in another world, his deeds are for all humankind in his world. This interpenetration of worlds constitutes the third trait of the fantasy genre.

Chapter Four

Another World

The third trait characterizing fantasy literature is the evocation of another world. This trait has received by far the most attention in critical circles and is perhaps the chief distinguishing trait of the genre. Scholars agree that writers create, or in Tolkien's term "subcreate," another world in which their characters live and move and have their being. By observing first several qualities of this other world in brief we may secondly explore its significance to a larger degree.

Traits of the Fantasy World

First, the world of fantasy matches our world in reality. It is not a dream world, a never-never land, but a world in which characters confront the same terrors, choices and dilemmas we confront in our world. The reason for creating such a world is to confront more openly and daringly a spiritual reality too often ignored in our world of system and fact. Eric Rabkin states that "although the dictionary may define the fantastic as 'not real or based on reality,' [*Random House Dictionary of the English Language*] the fantastic is important precisely because it is wholly dependent on reality for its existence. Admittedly, the fantastic is reality turned precisely 1ϵɾ around, but this is reality nonetheless, a fantasic narrative reality that speaks the truth of the human heart."[1]

Perhaps it is the case that when these "realities of the human heart" are devalued in our daily life, one must look to another world where such realities may be restructured and be given credibility and value. William Butler Yeats closed his moving poem "The Circus Animals' Desertion' with these lines:

> Now that my ladder's gone,
> I must lie down where all the ladders start,
> In the foul rag-and-bone shop of the heart.

I believe the author of fantasy is attempting to construct just such a ladder. When values seem fractured, one must begin with new structure; perhaps even the creation of a whole new world.

Second, this world is "evoked," or called forth clean and whole. It is simply provided for us, and we have to cross the threshold to it in our minds. Granted, some fantasies also provide such thresholds in the work—Lewis's wardrobe into Narnia, for example— but such devices are few and nonessential. Usually we are simply there in this other world from the first word. This immediacy is opposed, for example, to the nineteenth-century notion of "suspension of disbelief," with which we enter the work pretending for a time that this might be real. In fantasy, given a certain groundwork, the story *is* real. Rabkin comments that "Those who aren't willing to follow the signs in the text will throw down the book in distaste. Unless one participates sympathetically in the ground rules of a narrative world, no occurrence in that world can make sense—or even nonsense."[2]

C.N. Manlove, who has defined fantasy as "A fiction evoking wonder and containing a substantial and irreducible element of the supernatural with which the mortal characters in the story or the readers become on at least partly familiar terms,"[3] insists that the fantasy world is a "dramatic reversal" from ours. By this he means, I believe, that the fantasy world must be an internally consistent, but wholly other world. Unlike science fiction with its extrapolation from our world, the fantasy world is a mental leap *apart* from ours. In a brief article on Ursula Le Guin's *The Dispossessed,* Robert Scholes comments that Le Guin "Imagines other worlds rather than trying to extrapolate from our own."[4] This is precisely the case with all fantasy.

Third, the world of fantasy, however, should not be considered an escapist world, but a world in which we live. There is always this reciprocating action in fantasy, an interchange between two worlds. One of E. Nesbit's stories is entitled, all in one word, "Whereyouwanttogetto" and ends "Whereyoustartedfrom." Precisely: We leave the road of life for a time not to lose the road, but to find the road more certain. Eric Rabkin states the case thus: "In the literature of the fantastic, escape is the means of exploration of an unknown land, a land which is the underside of the mind of man."[5] In Le Guin's *The Dispossessed,* Shevek notes an epitaph on a tombstone reading: "To be whole is to be part; true voyage is return."[6] The cryptic statement encapsulates the meaning of much of Le Guin's fantasy work. Only when one is whole can he be a part of others; the only trip worth making is toward that wholeness, the return to self discovery.

It may also be the case, however, that if this other world is not real, by which many people mean not "measureable," it may nonetheless be true. In Saint Exupery's fantasy *The Little Prince* the narrator of the story is commanded by the Little Prince to draw a sheep.[7] The first sheep is unsatisfactory. It looks sickly and lifeless. The second too is unsatisfactory. In fact it has horns. It is a ram and not a sheep at all. When the third drawing also proves unsatisfactory, the frustrated artist draws a small box with holes in it. But where is the sheep? asks the Prince. Inside the box, the artist replies. Look. The Prince does look and this imaginary sheep is wholly up to expectation. The Prince proclaims, "Yes. I see the sheep, and it is sleeping." The imagination operates similarly in fantasy. If there is such a thing as extrapolation in fantasy, it is from the fantasy world to our own. The imagination sees the true thing in the other world.

The Making of the Other World

The foregoing, then, are several general qualities of the fantasy world. But what, we might ask, is its aesthetic relation to our world? What artistic properties come to bear upon the making of the fantasy world? The questions may be focused by an examination of J.R.R. Tolkien's significant essay "On Fairy-Stories," in which he considers the making of a fantasy world. In his essay, Tolkien moves from the mind of the maker to the meaning of that which is made. As such, the essay constitutes one of the few genuine aesthetic treatises on making a fantasy world. Taken together with examples of Tolkien's own artistic craft, the work does much to throw light on the nature of fantasy.

Considering that "the human mind is capable of forming mental images of things not actually present," Tolkien suggests that the imagination is simply this power of image-making.[8] To express these images that the human mind conceives, however, demands the talent of artistry. In aesthetic terms, Tolkien stands opposed to Benedetto Croce who described the aesthetic work simply as the idea-intuition. This is inadequate, Tolkien would respond, for the artist must possess the talent for shaping the image into an external form perceptible by others. To describe this talent, Tolkien borrows the neo-classical term "fantasy." The term was used by Addison, Johnson, and others to denote an intellectual faculty of conceiving pictorial representations. Tolkien extends the concept by arguing that fantasy is that "power of giving to ideal creations the inner consistency of reality" (p. 46). Fantasy arranges the image, and the artist's vision and beliefs, into a perceptible form.

Now, fantasy writers construct a special kind of form. Some forms of this talent may result in stream-of-consciousness, allegory, verisimilitude, beast fables; but others result in what Tolkien calls "Faerie," his equivalent for our term "fantasy." The literary artist of Faerie, for Tolkien, is a subcreator, one who constructs a secondary or "other" world which our mind can enter. Inside this world the artist places before us true things, which we believe, while inside the world. When disbelief arises, the spell is broken. It is not merely a case, as we have observed earlier, of the reader suspending disbelief, but a case of the artist sustaining enchantment. This the artist does through verbal artistry.

To effect the charm which lures and enchants us, the literary artist must observe certain formalities which give foundation to the successful world of the sub-creation. Primary among these is the necessity of "giving to ideal creations the inner consistency of reality" (p. 7). This the artist does by language. Tolkien himself had the rare gift for language which made a word absolutely appropriate to the emotional and mental circumstance. He speaks of his craft as "elvish," but it is much more concrete and prosaic than that. In short, his language is precise and deliberate to the circumstance at hand in the story. For example, when Bilbo Baggins descends into the heart of a mountain in *The Hobbit* he meets Gollum, that weird and sinister creature of the perpetual darkness. Gollum arises like primordial slime from the deep, dark recesses of an underground lake. His language is a hissing exhalation; an excess of slimy sibilants oozes out of his throat. Gollum is frightening, yet Tolkien manages to evoke a deep pathos for this poor creature, stranded without love and friendship in the bowels of the mountain.

Other stylistic traits than appropriate diction mark Tolkien's art. There is little straining in his prose, but rather a reliance upon the factual, declarative statement. The psychology here is important. We are accepted into this world, not coerced nor persuaded to enter. Perhaps one of the most famous stories of fantasy literature is how Tolkien, while grading examinations, came across an empty page and penned there the line which would open *The Hobbit*: "In a hole in the ground there lived a hobbit." A perfectly matter of fact statement. Accepted as apriori matter is not the fact that there are holes in the ground peopled by hobbits; but that there are hobbits and they naturally live in holes in the ground. Many writers would feel a compulsion to introduce their tale by explaining the nature of a hobbit. Tolkien spends the first paragraph explaining the hobbit's habitat: "Not a nasty, dirty wet hole, filled with the ends of worms and an oozy smell, not yet a dry, bare, sandy hole with nothing in it to sit down on or to eat: it was a hobbit-hole, and that means comfort."[9] If we accept the nature of the hole, it is only natural that a hobbit should inhabit it. Not until several paragraphs later does Tolkien raise the question what is a hobbit, and it is done in this mildly supererogatory manner: "The mother of our particular hobbit— what is a hobbit? I suppose hobbits need some description nowadays, since they have become rare and shy of the Big People, as they call us."[10] Notice that at no time does he call into question the actual existence of such a creature, rather he questions our memory of them. After this Tolkien brings us to the point where fairy-stories would start, the "once upon a time." This is Tolkien's rendition of the formula: "By some curious chance one morning long ago in the quiet of the world, when there was less noise and more green, and the hobbits were still numerous and prosperous, and Bilbo Baggins was standing at his door after breakfast smoking an enormous long wooden pipe that reached nearly down to his wooly toes (neatly brushed)—Gandalf came by."[11]

One finds later fantasy authors writing in this same straightforward manner. They assume a world, and then proceed to describe it. Richard Adams' *Watership Down,* for example, begins with this marvelously homely description:

> The primroses were over. Toward the edge of the wood, where the ground became open and sloped down to an old fence and a brambly ditch beyond, only a few fading patches of pale yellow still showed among the dog's mercury and oak-tree roots. On the other side of the fence, the upper part of the field was full of rabbit holes. In places the grass was gone altogether and everywhere there were clusters of dry droppings, through which nothing but ragwort would grow.[12]

Not until we are thoroughly familiar with the *place,* do we meet his characters. Similarly, Peter Beagle introduces *The Last Unicorn* with a flatly declarative statement:

> The unicorn lived in a lilac wood, and she lived all alone. She was very old, though she did not know it, and she was no longer the careless color of sea foam, but rather the color of

snow falling on a moonlit night. But here eyes were still clear
and unwearied, and she still moved like a shadow on the sea.[13]

A few paragraphs further Beagle tells us about unicorns, but it is
really unnecessary after having met one.

As with these other fantasy characters, in Tolkien's *The
Hobbit* we quickly discover our affinities with this creature,
discovering concomitantly the human in the hobbit and the
hobbit in the human. When the dwarves begin to arrive at Bilbo's
door, and begin to avail themselves of his courtesy, we begin also
to feel an uneasiness as the courtesy is nearly abused, and abuse
is an effective means of creating sympathy. The abuse is innocent
enough, and natural enough considering the nature of dwarves,
but the sympathy arises nonetheless.

Enough has been written about Tolkien's effective use of
words, that he was a lover of words who had a genius for making
his love real and effective. Tolkien was a gifted namer; of places,
people, and things. He possesses an ear for the sound which
matches the surrounding emotion; he caresses emotion from a
sound like a lover. Little has been said, however, about the utter
unpretentiousness of Tolkien's diction. He is appropriate with a
hard-nosed reality. Seldom will we find the flowers of
sentimentality blooming in Tolkien's prose. Nor is the diction
particularly difficult; but rather straightforward, an unfaltering
progression along with the emotional and physical place of the
novel.

Finally, the world which Tolkien sub-creates is a real world.
Not simply in the fantasy construction of meetings with talking
Eagles, Dragons, Elves, and Wizards which of course do not exist
in our pragmatic reality, but the spiritual meetings of man with
himself exemplified in such creatures. William Ready comments
that "It is to danger and turmoil, when Man realizes that the
Good is threatened, that he responds; the challenge is the spur."[14]
This is the real world of Tolkien's vision—the struggle for
spiritual confirmation and affirmation.

In brief, then, by means of his fitting simplicity of diction, his
appropriate naming, his skill in evoking mood by sound and
scene, his emphasis upon concerns which affect every man since
they are the concerns of the enduring spiritual dimension in
man's life, Tolkien has created an accessible world. It is a world
which both invites and directs the reader.

Properly achieved by literary artistry, the "elvish craft" of fantasy produces enchantment, and "Enchantment produces a Secondary World into which both designer and spectator can enter, to the satisfaction of their senses while they are inside: but in its purity it is artistic in desire and purpose" (pp. 52-53). This is the sub-creation, the secondary world.

Why a secondary world? To the mind of the fantasist, our primary world is one structured on routine and governed by fact—fact understood as "It is so." This world Tolkien calls the primary world. Contemporary existentialist philosophy has other names for it. Fantasists are more generous than the existentialist. In Rabkin's words: "The problem with the real world, frankly, is that it is the only one we have. To be sure, the real world is not an intolerably restricted world...."[15] But sometimes, Rabkin points out, "The real world is a messy place where dust accumulates and people die for no good reason and crime often pays and true love doesn't conquer much."[16] At such times, perhaps, we may prefer an order which art provides. About the fantasy world, Rabkin comments: "Such worlds are not merely *different* from our own, but *alternative* to our own. Fantastic worlds—perhaps paradoxically—are defined for us and are of interest to us by virtue of their relationship to the real world we imagine to have been thought normal when the story was composed."[17] To return to Tolkien's terms, in the sub-creation we engage a world of emotional conviction which is voiced not just by "It is so," but by "It is true." The "It is true" is the Amen to many things in fantasy; to friendship, to love, to adventure, to growing up in tests of experience, to the recognition of a struggle between good and evil, to many such things not reducible to quantifiable, factual formulae. Most importantly, for Tolkien, it is a lesson in Recovery, Escape, and Consolation.

Recovery, stated as simply as Tolkien put it, is the "regaining of a clear view" (p. 57). The goal of fantasy is not to convince us that there are ogres or elves in another world, but to lead us through the struggles of this other world to a better understanding of our own. Fantasy bestows upon us an experience of spirit which reveals to us certain truths with which to encounter our real world. Fantasy is a sojourn in faith; an assurance of things hoped for and things not seen. But the experience of this subcreated world endows us with a vision which orders our daily life in spiritual terms. We are called to the insight of what is good in a blinding confusion between good and evil. We engage life with a clarity of perspective, a "clearer view" which orders the demands of the age in accordance with the demands of the spirit.

Upon this realignment, these premises for belief and action, we come to a clearer understanding too of escape and escapism. Tolkien weighed this charge that he knew would be leveled against his art; that it is escapist literature: "I have claimed that Escape is one of the main functions of fairy-stories and since I do not disapprove of them, it is plain that I do not accept the tone of scorn or pity with which 'Escape' is now so often used: a tone for which the uses of the word outside literary criticism gives no warrant at all" (p. 60). To counter this charge Tolkien distinguished between the Escape of the Prisoner and the Flight of the Deserter. The Prisoner, says Tolkien, longs for his former daily life, for his home, his friends, his family, and "Why should a man be scorned if, finding himself in prison, he tries to get out and go home?" (p. 60). Fantasy creates an awareness of man's imprisonment in Process, of his slavery to daily fact which has stunted his spiritual life. With this recognition the Prisoner longs to return to his home and reorder his daily life. Fantasy affords the Prisoner this Escape—a liberation of spirit and meaning. Running counter to this view is the popular conception of the Flight of the Traitor; the man who forsakes his meaning. For the Prisoner who decides to "escape to life," awaits the expectancy of Consolation, or The Happy Ending. Within its artistic framework, fantasy provides an inkling of Consolation, that those who persevere and remain faithful to the vision are granted the joy of consolation. It is important to point out that Faerie, the realm of fantasy, does not deny sorrow. In fact, fantasy engages sorrow, fear, and trembling as the tests of faith. Fantasy leads us through difficulty as lessons on life's way to point us finally to the way of joy.

The Flight of the Traitor, argues Tolkien, begins with the failure to recognize sorrow and death as human agony, experiences also to be endured on life's way. The Traitor wants a Utopia; the Prisoner longs for life with all its attendant hardships. If we engage the struggle, we also engage the hope of Consolation; the hope that we, borne up by faith, will witness joy at the end of our earthly sojourn. There are two essential components of Consolation in Tolkien's view. First, the recognition of *dyscatastrophe,* a coinage by which he means the threat of sorrow and failure. And secondly, the *eucatastrophe,* by which he means the "fleeting glimpse of Joy, Joy beyond the walls of the world, poignant as grief" (p. 68). This joy in fantasy is the "sudden glimpse of the underlying reality or truth," which forms the underpinnings of our spiritual existence.

In his entire essay Tolkien is most emphatic in his belief that fantasy leads to joy. Complications must be resolved, harmony restored. Clearly, this sense of ultimate joy in fantasy is not a blithe daydreaming. Nor is it akin to the infinite abstraction that marked Romanticism, and German Romanticism in particular. While Holderlin longed for his "aether," Shelley for the tense flight of the skylark to lift him metaphysically beyond this world, Keats for the mystic, unseen nightingale fluting always a hill beyond one's present place, modern fantasy roots joy in this life. Complication and distortions are not merely *fled from*, they are actually resolved. Fantasy never denies the sorrow, even the horror, that is often close by the side of man. In fact, a common criticism of fantasy literature is that it is sometimes too brutally realistic. It is never realistic in the sense of many modern novels with their minute portrayals of seductions, aberrations, and mind-bending afflictions, but realistic in the psychological and spiritual battles that man has waged throughout his history. C.S. Lewis, for one, found himself defending his work against dilettantes who claimed that his work was too realistic. These works can't be for children, the charge went; they are too full of battles and blood, of homesickness and loneliness. Well, Lewis would respond, this is not psychologically remote from childhood. Moreover, the sense of having to fight for what is right and proper is not foreign to children. Their world is not a sheltered world, but a real world that is often nasty. It is on this point in particular that fantasy has outgrown its birthing-room in Romanticism.

Joy is, nonetheless, something longed for and fantasy does supply joy. Fantasy restores harmony and often in great festivity. The crowning touch of Tolkien's *Lord of the Rings,* the touch without which the entire trilogy would be incomplete, is the resolution which finally takes place after the great battles and upon the return to the Shire. After the terror of Mount Doom a certain universal order and joy is achieved. But finally it is made personal and poignant in the Shire with the routing of Saruman's influence. If there is a universal disruption in harmony which calls for great and terrible deeds, its effect will extend to all places. Here too harmony must be restored. The hobbits realize this after they finally defeat Saruman in their own lands:

'And that's the end of that,' said Sam. 'A nasty end, and I
wish I needn't have seen it; but it's a good riddance.'

'And the very last end of the War, I hope,' said Merry.

'I hope so,' said Frodo and sighed. 'The very last stroke. But
to think that it should fall here, at the very door of Bag End!
Among all my hopes and fears at least I never expected that.'[18]

Work remains, for harmony and peace don't come cheap. But all
the labor is worth the effort for it results in joy: the sense of being
home again spiritually as well as physically.

This is the sense of joy Harvey Cox has described as
"Festivity" in *Feast of Fools*. Western man, Cox writes, "while
gaining the whole world...has been losing his own soul. He has
purchased prosperity at the cost of a staggering impoverishment
of the vital elements of his life. These elements are *festivity*—the
capacity for genuine revelry and joyous celebration, and
fantasy—the faculty for envisioning radically alternative life
situations."[19] Festivity for Cox is "celebrative affirmation"
which entails saying yes to life. We might call it being at peace, or
possessing joy despite what travail comes our way. This,
according to Cox, fantasy provides in unique measure:

> Fantasy like festivity reveals man's capacity to go beyond the
> empirical world of the here and now. But fantasy exceeds festivity. In
> it man not only relives and anticipates, he remakes the past and
> creates wholly new futures. Fantasy is a humus. Out of it man's
> ability to invent and innovate grows. Fantasy is the richest source of
> human creativity. Theologically speaking, it is the image of the
> creator God in man. Like God, man in fantasy creates whole worlds
> *ex nihilo,* out of nothing.[20]

The significance of Tolkien's essay lies in the circular
movement from our primary world through the fantasy world of
the sub-creation and back to our primary world. Fantasy
construed as Tolkien does is therefore a means of engaging our
world of daily fact with renewed perspective and clarity of
insight. Fantasy is a wholly other world; but when successfully
constructed it holds securely the spirit of man.

We observe first, then, three qualities of the fantasy world:
that it matches our world in reality of truths expressed; that it is
evoked as a whole world, complete in its own geographical and
spiritual terms; and that it is not an escapist world but rather a

means of engaging the human spirit. Secondly, Tolkien provides an aesthetic basis for considering the fantasy world. The third issue that remains in our consideration of the fantasy world is the general significance or practical meaning of it. Can we locate an example here that is far-reaching and relevant enough to encompass fantasy generally? I believe that example may reside in Arthurian legend and specifically Alfred, Lord Tennyson's rendition of it. Consideration here will be given to the literary history of the legend since it is the basis for much modern fantasy, to Tennyson's particular use of it in response to his own age, and finally to Camelot and the metaphor of the city which occurs frequently in fantasy. If we are successful in this examination, we will understand more clearly the evocation of this other world, and its practical importance to our primary world.

The Arthurian Legend in Literary History

The legend of King Arthur is the premier and also the primordial fantasy. It partakes of all the qualities of fantasy literature and by its enduring nature has called to the mind of man for well over a millenium of literary history. Its permutations in literary history, how the legend intertwines with factual history, is necessary groundwork for consideration of the fantasy.

It goes without saying perhaps, how sacrosanct that story is in British history and legend. The legend had been embedded in the English mind for over a thousand years by the time of Tennyson's work. In *De Excidio et Conquesta Britanniae* (c. 540) Gildas recounted the heroic effort of Ambrosius Aurelianus to unite the people after the Saxon invasions. Important in Gildas' accounting is the uncertainty of the hero's parentage—which he describes simply as "undoubtedly of royal rank." With almost identical language Bede speaks of Ambrosius Aurelianus in Book I, Chapter 16 of *Historica Ecclesiastica Gentis Anglorum* (c. 731). With Nennius' *Historia Brittonum* (c. 800) Ambrosius, the victor of Mt. Badon in 516, becomes identified with Arthur, the King who in twelve great battles routed the Saxons. Nennius' active imagination heightens the supernatural aspects of Arthur as in Chapter 73 where he testifies to the ever-varying size of Arthur's sepulchre. By 1195 the power of the legend had grown to such an extent that a medieval equivalent of the modern demythologizer, Giraldus Cambrensis, saw fit to debunk the mystical passing of

Arthur to the Isle of Avilon by claiming to have found Arthur's body encoffined in a hollow oak. Nothing, perhaps, so indicates the power of a legend as the advent of the demythologizer.

The history is certainly clouded by the less than scientific hypotheses of early recorders. But it is in Romance and Chronicle that Arthur came to life, for here the skeleton held together by the historians' flimsy data was given flesh and blood. And it was from Romance that the huge symbolic significance of Arthur arose. Symbolism always originates in the physical thing to suggest a spiritual meaning. The Romances of the Middle Ages, for all their play upon an already confusing history, created the "real" Arthur. They created what Arthur signified, what he meant.

Friedrich Heer, one of the few contemporary historians to take seriously the *role* of Arthur in history (be the person real or legendary), speculates that the growth of that role in the 12th century may have been due in part as opposition to the furor over Charlemagne's canonization engineered by Frederick Barbarossa's anti-Pope. Only Arthur, argues Heer, "was of sufficient stature to stand in opposition to Charlemagne."[21] With the convenient discovery of Arthur's remains at Glastonbury, chronicled by Cambrensis, Richard I had the spiritual energies at hand to rally the English. Arthur, after all, represented God's emissary to man, and his people (for a time) rallied marvelously about him. So, at least, the chronicles of the Middle Ages would have us believe.

In "Culhwch and Olwen" (c.1100) of *The Mabinogion* Arthur is depicted as a sovereign well enthroned.[22] Despite the typical *Mabionogion* flurry of names (" 'It will be best,' said they, 'to seek Mabon, son of Modron, and there is no getting him until his kinsman Eidoel son of Aer is got first.' ") the story is a fascinating and often lively depiction, studded with warrior braggadocio, a great many windy threats, some outright bombast, and several minor heroic deeds.

It remained, of course, for Geoffrey of Monmouth in his *Historia Regum Brittanniae* (c. 1136) to give historical credence to Arthur and thereby open the door to the great medieval Arthurian legends. His chief contribution may simply have been his sorting out the kingship of Aurelius and Uther and the relation of Uther, Garlois, Igerna, and Arthur (In this account Arthur is the son of Uther Pendragon and Igerna—see Book VIII, Chapter 20). Geoffrey supplied the framework from which the mythmakers could fashion a real person. Unlike the *Mabinogion,* which had to account for every minor and wayward child in unlikely but entertaining lineages, Geoffrey gave the medieval writer confidence to say: That there was an Arthur is beyond disputation—here is what he was like; here is what he meant. Geoffrey made acceptable talk about wizards, grails, and other such oddities that the medieval mind lusted after. But these things above all Geoffrey provided:

> 1) The character of Arthur was indisputably noble, virtuous, piteous.
> 2) His deeds were valorous and unfailing in their integrity. The evil were destroyed; the good saved.
> 3) His governance was King as impeccable; a model of order, a byword for freedom, a design for others, a hope for the future. Tyrants . were driven out, freedom was established. Order prevailed.

The pattern was refined by Layamon (*Brut,* 1205), by the famous *Morte Arthures* (1360, 1400), by Malory's *Le Morte D'Arthur* (1469, 1485), but the models remained the same. Arthur's character grew. A public interest became a public obsession. England had its hero fit to rival Loki or Achilles. Chivalry was a *bona fide* religion, Arthur its high priest, the knights its mendicants, Guinevere its *intriguer.* Above all, Arthur was credited with creating a political order, a kingdom, out of the beast—the complete lack of order in which lawlessness and licentiousness reigned.

On the basis of this already rich and intricate legend, modern fantasists have found a wealth of material. Only a partial listing of influenced works may be mentioned here. Among the better known works are C.S. Lewis's *Space Trilogy,* a work that started as science fiction in *Out of the Silent Planet,* but became increasingly mythical and fantastic with the influence of Arthurian legend in the subsequent two volumes. By the last volume, *That Hideous Strength*, Lewis had included all the Arthurian trappings with the appearance of Merlin, the conflicting communities of Logres and Britain, and the establishment of Ransom as the Pendragon. Similarly, Lewis's fellow Inkling Charles Williams borrowed heavily from Arthurian legend. More recently we find Mary Stewart's trilogy; *The Crystal Cave, The Hollow Hills,* and *The Last Enchantment,* a fantasy retelling of the life of Merlin. Included on the list would be Susan Cooper's *Gray King* series for children, Lloyd Alexander's novels, T.H. White's familiar works, Evangeline Walton's work with the *Mabinogion,* and John Steinbeck's recent Arthurian novel. Particularly important here, however, is Alfred, Lord Tennyson's *Idylls of the King,* the most profound and powerful rendition of them all.

Arthur in the Nineteenth-Century

In 1858, Sir Henry Holland, writing for the *Edinburgh Review,* was searching for a phrase which would capture the spirit of Victorian England. What characterizes this period, he wrote, is "that we are living in *an age of transition.*"[23] Walter Houghton, in his remarkable study *The Victorian Frame of Mind,* amplifies Sir Henry's observation: "This is the basic and almost universal conception of the period. And it is peculiarly Victorian. For although all ages are ages of transition, never before had men thought of their own time as an era of change *from* the past *to* the future."[24] As proof for the validity of his claim, Houghton marshalls a host of writers who made use of the terms "transition" or "transitional" in regard to Victorian England, a list that includes: Prince Albert, Matthew Arnold, Disraeli, Bulwer Lytton, William Morris, John Stuart Mill, Carlyle, and Alfred, Lord Tennyson.

To be so keenly aware of transition may seem a curious sensibility to the modern mind, schooled as it is in a concept in which transition is the *status quo.* We get nervous if things don't change. We have adapted well to that situation which, to the Victorian mind, was reason for anxiety. The difference is this: we view change as the normal course of events living as we do on the far side of the industrial revolution. The Victorian mind perceived change as a threat to centuries of tradition that they saw as slipping away. Their perception was an acute sense of loss. At best, and perhaps at last, the Victorian hoped that he could retain with the tips of his clutching hands the spiritual values which this tradition had incarnated and retain those at least in his effort to confront the new age which loomed like leviathan.

In such an age, it seems a normal recourse for one to lament the fleeting past. But many Victorian thinkers sought earnestly to retain those spiritual values, and they looked to the past for models and patterns by which they could instill values in their own age. One such seeker was Alfred, Lord Tennyson, who in *Idylls of the King* revivifies the legendary kingdom of Arthur in an effort to find there models of kingship and political leadership which might be applicable to his age.

Few, I believe, were better equipped to speak to their age than Tennyson. For much of his life he struggled sincerely with whether to use his gift of making poetry or to follow his inclination toward politics. His life span, 1809-1892, covered the century. He was a close friend of and was respected by political leaders of the age. Moreover, as Poet Laureate of England he was in a very real sense representative of the established order. The *Idylls* are in fact dedicated to the memory of Prince Albert, Consort of the Queen.

But the *Idylls* does not exist as a mere paean to one political order. It exists rather as a poignant spiritual searching of the order of political justice in the lives of man. Joanna Richardson, in *The Pre-Eminent Victorian,* stated that:

> The *Idylls*...were one of Tennyson's most earnest, important attempts to deal with major contemporary problems. Through the Idylls he would affirm to his materialistic, doubting age, the ultimate reality of the spirit; he would show forth the kingship of the soul, and how only through that kingship the beast in man was subdued.... Man's true task, as Tennyson saw it, was to secure order and harmony in all phases of human activity: individual harmony, ordered by conscience; and social harmony expressed as a sense of justice, loyalty, duty, responsibility and love.[25]

This concept, which was fulfilled in the *Idylls,* was incipient in Tennyson's mind for much of his life. His son Hallam wrote in 1859 when the first four *Idylls* appeared that his father had carried "a more or less perfected scheme of them in his head over thirty years."[26] Tennyson's purpose in writing the *Idylls* was well spoken to by the poet himself. Hallam reports his father saying on his eightieth birthday: "My meaning in the *Idylls of the King* was spiritual."[27] And Tennyson wrote to John Knowles that "By King Arthur I always meant the soul, and by the Round Table the passions and capacities of a man."[28]

In the figure of Arthur, Tennyson explored the relationship between a political order and the liberty of mankind. To what extent must a political order go to insure the spiritual values of which Tennyson speaks? At what point does such an order impinge upon the freedom of the individual? The story of Arthur is a metaphor which developed Tennyson's political conceptions, but it also held up before the reading public a sense of past tradition which incarnated several of the ideals which Tennyson sought.

Given the general premise which Clyde de L. Ryals sets forth, and which I think is accurate, that "Nineteenth-century poetry seeks...to achieve this end: to illuminate the inner self by describing the external object, or in other words, to talk about oneself by talking about the object,"[29] then we should assume that Tennyson is talking about some inner state of man in the objective story of the *Idylls*. We understand, then, that Tennyson was working with a subject which was not only very much alive yet in the 19th century imagination, but also a subject richly suggestive in spiritual significance. Tennyson utilizes this ready-made framework to speak about his age. Particularly exigent, to Tennyson's mind, was the nature of political authority. These are some of the beliefs from fantasy, the "It is true," that he brings to the primary world, the "It is so."

First, Tennyson establishes that the kingdom is a gift and not a right. In many variations of the Arthurian legend the sword Excalibur, which is a symbol of ruling authority invested by God, is pulled by the young Arthur from a stone (see particularly Malory's *Morte*). In Tennyson's version the sword is given to Arthur by the mystic Lady of the Lake. The difference is important. The privilege to rule is not a right earned by the power of man. Might does not necessarily of itself make right; although the right may indeed be mighty. Rather than man seizing authority, the privilege to rule is a gift given to man. In Tennyson's vision the kingdom is a gift to be ordered for a time according to divine mandates which insure liberty for the members of the kingdom.

Second, in the tradition of the medieval legend in which the *Idylls* are rooted, we perceive the development of the *comitatus,* the band of men swearing unfailing loyalty (*liege*) to their leader. Since his authority is given by an absolute authority, the heroic character, spiritual insight, and leadership ability of the king seem beyond the reach of his followers. As Tristram says of Arthur, "Every follower eyed him as a God." The point is that he is a leader; not a legislator. From the Round Table, which is for Tennyson "image of the mighty world," the knights might dispense the centralized vision into all the world. Thereby the idea of liberty and right deeds is ordered in effective political machinery.

Third, the expectation of the King is that his vision of harmony and order which is established in Camelot will in fact transform the world, bringing dark places under the influence of the radiant vision, driving back the beast of disorder by the strong sword of order.

Uncomfortable questions arise to the modern reader. Is Tennyson's vision hopelessly idealistic? Is this anachronism dredged up from the middle ages a viable model? It is necessary to remind ourselves that Tennyson is seeking a spiritual symbol first of all, and not a political order *per se*. He would not have knights in trolley cars nor kings on white chargers. Like his stormy contemporary Thomas Carlyle, who argued in *Sartor Resartus* that the modern spiritual temper must be revivified by retailoring our spiritual symbols, Tennyson ushers a call for spiritual revision. His belief is that this revision is not initiated by laws or bureaucracies, but rather by authoritative leadership. Models for such leadership, if lacking in this world, may be established in another world.

Camelot as Other World and as Metaphor

One of the primary distinguishing traits of fantasy, as we are arguing here, is the evocation of another world; yet this other world, this community, is not one which is improbable in terrestrial terms but rather one which is possible in spirit. The expectation is that the revelation of this fantasy community may provide impetus and direction for ordering terrestrial affairs.

Since this other world constructed in fantasy contains paradigmatic spiritual realities, insights into abstract truths which may be translated into practical reality in our world, it is absolutely essential that such insights focus on a place, a specific locus of meaning. In fantasy literature this place is often represented by the "sacred city," a fount from which the spiritual center of meaning may flow outward among mankind. The city thus represents the unifying force among the people, but also the generative force which invests their lives with direction and meaning.

We find such a city, for example, on the Isle of Roke in Ursula Le Guin's *Earthsea Trilogy*. Roke is the locus of spiritual meaning in the world of Earthsea, a place which is visited with supernatural presence and against which the forces of darkness cannot prevail. But Roke is also the point from which spiritual direction radiates out into the larger world. As the advanced training school of the most learned and powerful spiritual leaders in the land, Roke extends its influence into all surrounding regions. However, because of the foremost sacredness of the place, it is also certain that a rupture within the sacred city itself will absolutely affect all territories under the influence of that city. Thus, when young Ged summons the spirit of darkness in the heart of Roke, permitting a rupture in the city itself, this immediately jeopardizes all surrounding territory. If the sacredness of the holy place is honored, a principle for order is revered and sustained in the land. If the center cannot hold, the gyre falls apart.

In *The Idylls of the King,* we see the establishment of the sacred city in Camelot. While my concern here will be specifically with the nature of Camelot as spiritual center for Arthur's kingdom, the pattern which Tennyson establishes is one often repeated in fantasy work and illustrative of the role of the city.

Consider first Arthur's vision for the kingdom. Arthur's stated purpose is to locate the kingdom of God on earth, to create a human means which will serve as effective instrument for God's will. The kingdom does not emanate from man for man, but rather it emanates from a transcendent power revealed among men. This is seen particularly in "Gareth and Lynette" of the *Idylls.* When the young Gareth approaches Camelot, he goes in disguise and engages in a deceit to gain entrance. He is met along the way by amazed travelers who relate that the city is only a dream:

> Here is a city of enchanters, built
> By fairy kings.

And

> Lord, there is no such city anywhere,
> But all a vision.[30]

The central issue is whether the vision can be incarnated in physical reality, or whether it is merely a dream.

The city described by Tennyson is a marvelously intricate affair whose walls are guarded by runes and whose entrance is gained by "a living gate."[3] At the gate stands Merlin and for him the city is something always growing; like music evolving in ever-new harmonies:

> They are building still, seeing the city is built

> To music, therefore never built at all,
> And therefore built forever.

Two important points are revealed by Merlin. First, the city cannot be identified finally with the secular structure, but can be seen *in* it. The city is abstract, a vision which guides temporal events. Secondly, although kingdoms may rise and fall which to a greater or lesser degree incarnate the vision, the vision itself never diminishes. It is eternal.

This lesson is one which Arthur learns with great pain. He does for a time envision the city as an enduring presence on earth, as if the city were the primary thing and not the vision which it manifests for a time. His lesson is precisely that "the old order changeth, yielding place to new." Yet, for a time, he earnestly believes that he can establish the city in finality on earth. The danger of the city is that the dynamism of the spiritual vision may become merely a codification of rigid laws. Unwilling to live always on the dangerous edge of fulfilling the spiritual presence on earth, man has a desire to codify that eternal, abstract presence into readily apparent tables of law.[31] In Arthur's kingdom this occurs in his swearing of his knights to "so strait vows." The vows initially are an idealistic commitment to the quest to reveal God's will in the world. In time the vows become an end in themselves. In "The Last Tournament" Tristram acknowledges that "The vow that binds too strictly snaps itself," and admits that:

> They served their use, their time; for every knight
> Believed himself a greater than himself,
> And every follower eyed him as a God.

When the vow itself becomes an end, we have merely system and not vision.

That Camelot represents Tennyson's vision of an ideal political order, governed by divine will, is likely one of the best attested themes in literary criticism. As we observed in the immediately preceding section, Tennyson affirms that the kingdom is a gift and not a right, that the leader's vision is disseminated through his government, and that the purpose of the kingdom is to establish harmony and order in the world at large. By extension, the city or seat of the kingdom represents: 1) the unfolding revelation of divine direction for life, 2) the human means for effecting the vision, 3) the task toward which these means must be directed—driving out disorder and darkness and supplanting the beast with harmonious order.

In modern fantasy this metaphorical pattern frequently prevails. For example, the twentieth-century fantasist Charles Williams was powerfully attracted by this multiple representation of the sacred city. In his specifically Christianized Arthurian tales, he described the political order as a human body, patterned in part on St. Paul's analogy of "one body" in Romans 12: 4-8. In "The Vision of the Empire" of *Taliessin through Logres,* the city is the "organic body" singing together in harmony. For Williams, Camelot is simply one manifestation of this ever-changing city which is designated by him as Logres, a term taken to mean the manifestation of the Logos in temporal government:

> In the season of Midmost Sophia
> the word of the Emperor established a kingdom in Britain;
> they sang in Sophia the immaculate conception of wisdom.
>
> Carbonek, Camelot, Caucasia,
> were gates and containers, intermediations of light;
> geography breathing geometry, the double-fledged Logos.[32]

Williams figuratively places Logres, the locus of God's immanent rule on earth, as the head of the body politic. Logres is the impelling force in the spiritual design, the human means by which God works out his kingdom in the affairs of men.

In fantasy literature, whether the sacred city be specifically Christianized or not, it nonetheless represents the locus of order in the affairs of the kingdom, a center from which forces of darkness and disorder may be driven back, and a spiritual harmony arranged by supernatural powers but revealed in the affairs of men.

In the pattern of the *Idylls,* however, there is always a threat to this harmonious order. The threat is first of all an external one, what Tennyson designates collectively as "the beast." And, although my effort here is to show a pattern which may be applicable to later fantasy works, it is readily evident that there must be some tension between the sacredness of the city and the bestiality of the opposing force that threatens the city in fantasy literature. One of the characteristic traits of the genre is a struggle between opposing forces, more often than not forces clearly representing good and evil. For example, in C.S Lewis's *That*

Hideous Strength, we find juxtaposed to the small enclave Logres the terrible power of Britain, a juxtaposition which Lewis borrowed from Williams. In Le Guin's *Earthsea Trilogy* we find Roke constantly threatened by the ever-encroaching forces of darkness until at last the Mage Ged must go out into darkness itself to do battle with it. In *The Children of Llyr* from Evangeline Walton's *Mabinogion* series, the city Harlech on the Island of the Mighty is threatened by the deeds of the sinister Matholuch, the Irish King.

But in each instance the external threat is preceded by an internal fracture in the order itself. In *The Children of Llyr* it is preceded by the "journey of Penardim the Dark Woman, the mother of the Sons of Llyr," and her rape by Eurosswydd which leads to internal struggle among her children. The struggle between Evnissyen and Nissyen, incidentally, parallels the struggle between Balin and Balan from the Arthurian legend. While under the strong influence of the ordered kingdom their tragically juxtaposed personalities may be kept in balance; when exposed to the outer world, the land of the beast, they are destructive of each other and all around them,

In Tennyson's *Idylls* we notice that the internal threat occurs on several levels. First and most obvious is the destructive relationship between Guinevere and Lancelot. Guinevere always represented for Arthur more than a simply physical relationship. She, and their marriage, were to embody the *agape,* the spiritual order of the kingdom:

> For saving I be join'd
> To her that is the fairest under heaven,
> I seem as nothing in the mighty world,
> And cannot will my will nor work my work
> Wholly, nor make myself in mine own realm
> Victor and lord. But were I join'd with her,
> Then might we live together as one life,
> And reigning with one will in everything
> Have power on this dark land to lighten it.

While it is not my intention here to pursue fault in the disintegration of their marriage, whether it be Guinevere's love for Lancelot, or Arthur's failure by his idealization of Guinevere to be wholly appreciative of her as a woman, it is my contention that the internal rupture of their marriage is a human flaw in the ideal vision which finally serves to fracture that vision. The implication is that humankind is still partially but decisively on the side of the beast, that the beast has a grip on human nature.

But even this may be dealt with. Although the nature of man may be irremediably tainted by the beast, it is not therefore irremediable. If the spiritual order is seen as a dynamic, ever-changing presence, as the *Idylls* testifies, then it cannot and must not be allowed to become merely static codification of law. The huge internal failure of Arthur's Camelot is that the vision, which is essentially abstract in nature, becomes identified *with* the physical order. The spiritual vision was transplanted by the "so strait vows," to a degree that the vows were an end in themselves. The vision cannot solidify into a rigid codebook. The sacredness is the vision symbolized by the city, not the city itself. What we can affirm about the nature of the sacred city by an examination of Tennyson's *Idylls of the King,* then, is this. The city is established by supernatural powers, a gift to man for man to direct for a time and not a right earned by man alone. While it is true that the authority of the city may be established by mighty deeds, represented by Excalibur, governance of the city is not attained by deeds alone, but only by those deeds consonant with the spiritually directed vision.

While the city functions according to divinely revealed mandate, "to do His will" as Arthur says, the city functions as both metaphor for the divinely inspired harmony of the world and as a locus of meaning from which this harmony may radiate outward to order the affairs of man, to drive back the beast that threatens this order.

In temporal affairs of men, the city may not be allowed to become mere symbol, so that the living, abstract animus of the city is lost. The city is a tableland between two deeps, and as Arthur says: "I pass but shall not die." The spiritual vision must be ever-renewed, must not be allowed to degenerate to mere human law. Threatening the city, and the reason for this living vision rather than a dead code-book of law, is the fact that while evil may be driven back for a time it is in fact always there, always to be dealt with. New weapons must always be forged in the crucible of human crisis.

This threat, finally, may be seen as two kinds. The external threat is always most evident. Britain, as Lewis said in his analysis of Williams' *Taliessin,* grows ever larger, often to the point where Logres seems a fragile little community on the point of extinction. Wars shall not cease; the enemy seems to grow ever stronger. But the beast is also evidenced internally. The debasement of *Agape* to *Eros*, of love to lust, of obedience to infidelity, evidenced here in Guinevere and Lancelot, is a beast which rears its raging head in the heart of every man. Law may keep the beast in check; commitment to the compelling vision may subdue it; but always the beast is there.

In conclusion, I should like to remark that Tennyson's vision of the sacred city is not therefore one of pessimism or despair, but rather one of affirmation and hope. This trait also characterizes modern fantasy. The secular city seems to grow even stronger, but the belief fantasy holds forth is that the sacred city, although battered and torn, will never die out. It will endure. And the inhabitants of that city always believe that it, and the values it holds forth, will one day come into fullness.

Chapter Five

Magic and the Supernatural:
Good and Evil

The linking of two generic traits in one chapter is not merely for the sake of convenience. The two are inextricably related. C.N. Manlove has argued that the use of the supernatural is not simply a "possibility" in fantasy; it is the driving force in the story and takes a central role in the development and shaping of characters as well as plot. But, as I will argue here, the actions of these characters in the plot have ethical implications. The use of magic and supernatural powers inevitably turns actions to good or evil significance. In his fine study entitled *The Fantasy Tradition in American Literature,* Brian Attebery observes that:

> High fantasy establishes a sphere of significance, in which the actions of hero and inhuman, helper or villain, reflect a coherent and extractable order. Characters are not merely individuals but the upholders of moral and intellectual standards.[1]

As was established in the discussion of heroism, the character in fantasy literature stands for a community. By his commonness he is representative of humankind. By virtue of so standing in representation, this character's actions also represent the values of the community. While the fantasy hero is often a lonely hero, even isolated from humankind, at no time should this hero be confused with the self-imposed exile of the existential anti-hero. The anti-hero imagines himself in a moral vacuum, the executor of a self-chosen and self-sufficient world of choices. The fantasy hero must choose, but his choices have repercussions beyond himself and he is keenly aware of this *before* choosing. But neither are the fantasy hero's choices governed by Heidegger's specifically derogatory sense of fallenness [Verfallenheit], in which the individual is so structured by social norms that he has forsaken free choices. The fantasy hero, it must be made clear, is individually free to choose, *must* choose, but his choices have consequence far beyond the confines of his one life.

Magic and the presence of supernatural powers, then, are in fantasy inescapably allied with the problem of good and evil. Some preliminary investigation of these terms is in order. First, magic and the supernatural are terms which I shall use nearly interchangeably to connote the presence of powers whose origins and nature lie outside of human knowledge or common experience.

In fantasy literature magic takes on two forms. In the tradition known as "high fantasy" the supernatural or magical power provides much of the driving impetus of the story. The story is, if you will, about magic and how it affects man. In such fantasy these powers are always mysterious to man, but by certain rites, incantations, or motions, can be drawn upon by man and used to human ends. In Le Guin's *A Wizard of Earthsea* the mage Ogion says to young Ged:

> 'Ged, listen to me now. Have you never thought how danger must surround power as shadow does light? This sorcery is not a game we play for pleasure or for praise. Think of this: that every word, every act of our Art is said and is done either for good, or for evil. Before you speak or do you must know the price that is to pay!'[2]

In such fantasy powers of good or evil are controlled by man. Further, there is a sense of balance between such powers, an equilibrium. Man can tip the balance for good or evil.

In high fantasy, moreover, there is a deliberate ranking of mortals in relation to their control over magical powers. Essentially, in ascending order of control, the heirarchy may be arranged thus. The most common, and lowest level of magician is the *witch* whose power is usually limited to the making of certain concoctions. There is power locked in things; in the herbs, the flowers, in certain trees especially. These things the witch knows and is able to use, although the witch's knowledge of the power underlying those things is severely limited. Usually the witch's power has authority only in small, rural areas susceptible to the witch's wiles. Her concoctions may serve as curatives or debilitations. Second on the heirarchy is the *sorcerer* who has the ability, through certain incantations or rituals, to unlock deeper powers that underlie things. The sorcerer, for example, is able to perform more profound magic than the witch such as calling forth the "werelight," the small globe of light from out of darkness. The sorcerer has an inherent bent (which he or she cannot escape) to use this power in a good or bad way; hence the term "white" or "black" sorcerer. The *wizard*, on the other hand, understands the nature of the power itself and therefore has a keener understanding of the implications for use of that power. The wizard knows quite certainly what powers lead to evil and which to good, but his understanding of the power enables him to choose one or the other. The wizard may be "bent" toward evil when his greed for power overrules judicious use of power. The *mage*, the highest member of the magical heirarchy, is a ruling authority. While all the powers of the others have decided implications for the lives of those surrounding them, the mage has authority because of deep understanding, because of designated rule, and because of power, to order the very lives of the magicians.

In each instance, however, we observe that man can effect good or evil by his actions. In the second form of magic in fantasy, we find in many authors a distaste for what in the above appears to be a Manichaean dualism in which good and evil are in conflict, but the conflict is resolved by the choices and actions of man. In light of this, this second camp of authors establishes the view that the power of evil is limited, and that the power of good is the absolute authority which sets the limits. Evil does wield a certain power when, through rites, incantations, or motions, man allows himself to become a receptacle for such power to exercise itself. But the power of good is always seen as the prior and absolute power. Such power is not dependent upon human nature but always works directly. In fact, man is often surprised at the appearance of such power. It lies beyond his expectation and comprehension. Because this power lies wholly beyond man's control, man sometimes describes it by the adjective "magical" simply to indicate the fact that he does not understand it. One might also use the word "miraculous."

A second affirmation follows upon that above. In all fantasy literature there is a keen recognition of forces of good and evil, a sense of right and wrong; but also a driving necessity to act upon it. It may be the case, however, that in the human struggle of the character to act upon choices between good and evil the distinction may become blurred. Often he does not know for certain if his action is correct *until* he has acted. Often the choice must be construed from what appears to human perspective as a gray area, and it is precisely such a choice, as Robert Browning demonstrated in *The Ring and the Book,* that constitutes "life's terrible choice." The German poet Goethe, distressed by the obscuring of actions by words which empty action of significance, rephrased the first chapter of the Gospel of John to read: "In the beginning was the deed." And so too in fantasy. One must act to see clearly. The act itself may be committed in great tension and uncertainty, but it is only by acting that one may arrive at certainty.

Fantasy is keenly aware of the terror of life as well as the joy of life. But like the fairy tale, fantasy does hold forth as one of its central points the belief that the end of a successful story is joy. It is not a joy separate from sorrow, but a joy distilled from the experience of agonizing choice and painful awareness of the errors in human decision making. Only through such decisions and the actions attendant upon them, may the often hazy edges of good and evil be clarified.

This contrast between fantasy and "high fantasy" on the use of magic is an important one currently. The distinction may be made clearer by contrasting in closer analysis a well-known work from each type and the uses of magic employed in each. Consider first C.S. Lewis's *The Magician's Nephew* and then Ursula Le Guin's *A Wizard of Earthsea.*

The Magician's Nephew: Mage and Maker

Lewis sets forth in *The Chronicles of Narnia* a carefully refined pattern of distinctions between magic, which is essentially human manipulation of supernatural forces, and the absolute authority of Aslan which frequently appears incomprehensible to human understanding. The distinction here is between the "Mage," the magician who attains power by secret rituals or incantations, and the "Maker" whose word is absolute authority. For our purposes here, I use the term "Mage" not in its high fantasy hierarchy but generally to describe any manipulation of magical powers. That the power of magic is real Lewis never doubts. That its power is only within the limits permitted by the absolute sovereign he assiduously attests.

The pattern of Mage and Maker is most clearly asserted in *The Magician's Nephew* and provides a significant motif throughout the tales. In *The Magician's Nephew* we encounter magical power initially through Uncle Andrew, an ingenue in the practice who views magic simply as manipulation without an understanding of its power ("Uncle Andrew, you see, was working with things he did not really understand: most magicians are"), and also through Queen Jadis, who appears as the White Witch in *The Lion, the Witch and the Wardrobe.*

Andrew is representative of mere human understanding of magical power—a greedy effort to attain control which will benefit the user. In the history of religions one discovers that many ancient religions were based precisely on this belief. For example, Canaanite Baal-Worship was based on the myth of the dying and rising god Baal, god of fertility, who was slain by Mot, god of drought. By the proper incantations and rituals, including sacred prostitution and occasionally child sacrifice, at the altar of Baal, the Canaanites believed they could manipulate divine powers and enable Baal to ascend the throne and insure a fertile crop.

Andrew had inherited an Atlantean box from his "fairy" godmother, one Mrs. Lefay (*le fay* means "the fairy"). The box contained otherworldly matter from which Andrew fashioned the rings. In effect, the rings are accidental to him, and he experiments blindly with them. Andrew recognizes only that they possess powers beyond human knowledge—and in his tortured, materialistic mind power is equated with wealth. In fact, Andrew is wholly incorrigible from this view. Even after witnessing the creation of Narnia by Aslan's singing, to which his greed has made him physically deaf and spiritually blind, Andrew can see in it only fascinating "commercial possibilities." Magic is always oriented about the individual, the possessor of power, and that at the expense of other's welfare. Of such people, the narrator remarks, "They are not interested in things or people unless they can use them."[3] So it is that Andrew must trick the children into using the rings, utterly unconcerned about their welfare.

Magic, therefore, may be considered a kind of gnostic key to unlock power. Queen Jadis sees the "marks" of the magician on Andrew, but is baffled how such a low, common sort should come by them. Magic in her view belongs only to royal blood ("who ever heard of common people being Magicians"), since only those with power are fit to possess the greater power of magic.

In fantasy tradition, this power is ethically relativist. Magic itself is indiscriminate as to good or evil, but is simply available to those who know how to possess it. Given such power, in Lewis's view, fallen man will only use it in a fallen manner. As such, magic in the hands of man is used for evil purposes. It is thereby destructive rather than constructive. Faced with the creative power of Aslan, the Maker, the Witch "hated it. She would have smashed that whole world, or all worlds, to pieces, if it would only stop the singing" (101). This recalls the paradox of the ring in J.R.R. Tolkien's *The Hobbit* and *Ring Trilogy*. Only a perfect being can wear the ring, but a perfect being has no need for such a ring. In the *Trilogy* the ring gives absolute power, which in the hands of fallen creatures permits unlicensed evil.

I remarked that in the tradition of fantasy the power obtained by magic is ethically relativist. By this I mean that the power itself is considered morally neutral. The use of the power by humans may be to good or evil ends. Thus, in the tradition of fantasy we find so-called "white" magicians and so-called "black" magicians; those who exercise the neutral power to good ends or bad ends respectively. This dualism was discomforting to Lewis. While he makes some concessions to the fantasy tradition in *The Chronicles,* I have found no evidence, either in Lewis's apologetics or fiction, to suggest any belief in a "neutral field" of supernatural power. It seems quite evident instead that Lewis sees supernatural powers of only two sorts: good or evil. This may be clearly seen, I believe, in *The Space Trilogy,* as well as *The Chronicles* as a whole. How, then, do we reconcile this with Lewis's use of the tradition in fantasy that magic is a neutral power? First of all, Lewis makes use of the traditional genre to serve his own purposes. What may initially appear to be a neutral power in *The Magician's Nephew* clearly becomes defined by the end of the book in terms of good or evil. But secondly, one might say that the rituals or incantations, instead of enlisting the aid of a neutral power, in fact open one up to, or invite, an evil power. The ritual, then, becomes not the tool which controls the power, but the gateway by which the evil power possesses the person. As we will see in this investigation, the power of good has absolutely no need of such intermediary devices. Moreover, for Lewis such a view would be consonant with biblical teaching on magic, particularly with those Old Testament passages which inveigh against the ritual or incantation itself.

In *The Magician's Nephew* Lewis presents his clearest contrast between the purposes and effects of Mage and Maker. While the magician manipulates supernatural powers for self gain, the Maker brings acts and physical things into being by his own power and for the benefit of others. The power of the Maker is *not* dependent upon any external paraphernalia. The magician must rely upon devices (Andrew's rings), rituals (the worship of Tash in *The Last Battle*), or incantations (Jadis's powerful "deplorable word"). Aslan calls directly. The power is in him, through him only. His power is inherent to his being and illimitable. Thus, when Queen Helen is called to Narnia in *The Magician's Nephew*, she is called directly and immediately: "Fetched out of our world not by any tiresome magic Rings, but quickly, simply, and sweetly as a bird flies to its nest" (137). To the children Aslan says: "You need no Rings when I am with you" (177). Moreover, his power is there for the simple asking and in the simplicity of faith in its efficacy. It is not a power that can be bartered or bargained for, but is absolute and free. One has only to ask Aslan for it, but one must ask.

The power of the Maker is absolute power. We notice that magic, since it is relative to the manipulator, is limited in its time and place of efficacy. Jadis's spells are not effective on earth. Her horrible imprecations there raise only the observation from Miss Ketterley that "The woman is drunk. Drunk! She can't even speak clearly" (80). Yet, Aslan's power extends to all worlds. Magic is given more latitude in some lands than others, but its power is always within the limits permitted by the absolute authority of the Maker. Jadis clearly understands this overarching sovereignty and comprehends before the humans the true nature of Aslan's power: "But the Witch looked as if, in a way, she understood the music better than any of them. Her mouth was shut, her lips were pressed together, and her fists were clenched. Ever since the song began she had felt that this whole world was filled with a Magic different from hers and stronger" (100).

In light of this dialectic between Mage and Maker, one wonders: What does one gain from magic? Why would one desire it? The Mage gains power. Under Aslan's absolute authority one must learn obedience. This power humbles one. This is not to say that one becomes a slave to it, but rather that one holds such authority in awe and reverence, recognizing it as the "wholly other" manifested among men. Before such authority one must learn obedience. Digory recognizes this even while still trying to comprehend the true nature of Aslan's authority: "He realised in time that the Lion was not at all the sort of person one could try to make bargains with" (141). Realizing the power of such authority, one places his life under the rule and guidance of this authority. In *The Magician's Nephew* Digory fulfills the command of Aslan and the mission is essentially one in learning obedience. At the door of the sacred garden from which Digory is to bring an apple stands a golden gate bearing this inscription.:

> Come in by the gold gates or not at all,
> Take of my fruit for others or forbear.
> For those who steal or those who climb
>   my wall
> Shall find their heart's desire and find
>   despair.

In sum, the inscription testifies to the way of obedience. The precious treasure is guarded by an absolute authority, but that authority has also constructed a clear pathway to the treasure. As the power of the Maker is to restore others to wholeness, so the fruit of the garden is to help others. If this is abrogated by personal desire one finds only despair.

This motif may be traced at greater length throughout the *Chronicles*. I should like simply to focus upon this final aspect of obedience in Lewis's conception a bit further: both Mage and Maker demand subjection—but the subjection of the Mage is to abject servility while that of the Maker is to a recognition of place and purpose in life which grants meaning and direction for life. This theme is recaptured in *The Lion, the Witch and the Wardrobe* in which Jadis appears again as the White Witch whose relentless power has spread and encased Narnia in a rule of icy slavery.

Jadis is perhaps one of Lewis's most complex mythic characters, comparable to the heroine Psyche of *Till We Have Faces* in her mythological background. In *The Lion, the Witch and the Wardrobe* Jadis the White Witch is alluded to by Mr. Beaver as Adam's first wife Lilith. The derivation of the name is from the Jewish Cabala in which a mystical effort is made to appease seeming contradictions in the Torah. Genesis 1:27 reports that "God created man in His own image, in the image of God He created him: male and female He created them." Apparently the verse asserts that *male* and *female* were created at this point. Yet not until Genesis 2:18f is recorded the creation of Eve, "She shall be called Woman, because she was taken out of man." The passage has created theological difficulties for biblical scholars. One theory of interpretation argues that Chapter 2 of Genesis is a pause in the creation account which fills in the gaps of the quick-paced and lyrical description of Chapter 1. Thus verses 5 and 8 of Chapter 2 fill in the gap between Chapter 1, verses 11 and 12 by describing the effoliation of vegetable life.

Similarly, verses 18-25 of Chapter 2 fill in the gaps of verse 27 of Chapter 1 by giving a detailed account. In effect, Chapter 1 sketches a skeletal framework, and Chapter 2 fleshes it out. The mystical method of the Cabala interjects a folklore element to explain the two accounts of woman's creation. The folk tale suggests that Adam's first wife (Chapter 1:27) was an angelic being of female sex. This spiritual mate was not "suitable" (viz. 2:18) for the physical Adam, and therefore a physical mate, Eve, was created to replace her. Angered and jealous over this, the angelic mate Lilith pledges herself to disturbing the children of Eve—children she could not bear. Thus Lilith is depicted as the tormentor of all the children of Eve. In later Medieval times Lilith is depicted as a vampire visiting children as they slept. The associaton may be influenced also by the Assyrian myth of Lilitu, the demon which haunted dark places.

For Lewis's purposes in *The Lion, the Witch and the Wardrobe,* Jadis is imaged as Lilith by the Beavers because she has sworn vengeance upon the sons of Adam and daughters of Eve. Her reign of evil was secure until such humans should appear in the kingdom, and their arrival was signification of the coming of Aslan and the destruction of her reign.

Jadis enforces her reign by enchantment, by magic, and the various living beings she has encased in ice bear mute witness to the effects of magic upon the human spirit. Jadis's magic, we discover, goes back in power to the "Dawn of Time," which I take to mean the creation of earth (or the pre-Narnian lands in the *Chronicles*), although some scholars see it as Satan's fall from heaven. The reason I prefer the creation of earth as the "Dawn of Time" and extent of Jadis's power, is that the power is thereby concurrent with the fallen angel's victory over man and thus evil's gaining of a substantial foothold in God's kingdom. Such a view is also true to the history of Narnia. Although Jadis's power pre-existed Narnia, the efficacy of her power there extends to the creation account in *The Magician's Nephew,* and specifically to her eating of the forbidden fruit in the sacred garden.

The crucial factor here is that this foothold gained by evil in the world has limits in Lewis's view, and these limits are precisely circumscribed by Aslan's power—the Deep Magic from Before the Dawn of Time. Alsan is the Maker, the creator *ex nihilo.* The Mage has power only within the created order. The power of the Maker calls into being; the power of the Mage works to pervert the being which the Maker has created.

Since the power of the Maker is the primary power, it extends throughout his kingdom. When the true believers seek the power of the Maker, the power of the Mage weakens. When one seeks in obedience, the shackles of servility begin to snap.

However, since the power of evil has gained considerable power indeed, one fails to fully comprehend the absolute power of Aslan's, or the Maker's, authority. Thus Aslan's exercise of authority is frequently imaged in terms of magic. For example, the children feel the pull of "magic" each time they are called to Narnia. Similarly, the use of Susan's horn to call aid in time of dire need seems a magical device. But these should not be considered the tools of magical trade for Lewis. They are emblems of Aslan's authority which he has granted to man to bestow upon them the assurance of his presence.

In conclusion, then, Lewis has constructed clear distinctions between Mage and Maker. These distinctions are based on the following: the use of intermediary devices as opposed to direct call; the lust for power as opposed to obedience.

It is obvious that Lewis's fictional world is governed by his theological presuppositions; and it is equally clear that his view of magic and good and evil is shared not just by his fellow Inklings, particularly Tolkien and Williams, but by a host of other fantasists. These would include those not of Lewis's theological orthodoxy, but those who are adamant in the belief that the good is a preexistent power from which evil is a warping or deviation. Equally strong in the genre, however, is the bent toward high fantasy which views the issue in slightly different terms. A premier writer and exemplar of this tradition is Ursula K. Le Guin. Her *Earthsea Trilogy* provides a fine basis for comparison and contrast to Lewis's *Chronicles* for several reasons. Important comparisons inhere in the works themselves. Both are ostensibly directed toward a youthful audience. Both have been read by millions of adults with keen enjoyment. This is as much to say, perhaps, that both are fine works of art. Both works deal with youthful protagonists receiving their initiation into another world. While Lewis transports his children to the other world, Le Guin evokes her world of Earthsea immediately. Most importantly, both works are about magic, its use and effects. But what difference do the different views of the author toward magic and good and evil make for the work itself? This immediate difference: since Lewis believes in the ultimacy of the good, incarnated in Aslan, the good responds to and assists the protagonist in his heroic endeavors. In high fantasy, there is no such clear response. Since the protagonist *controls the magical powers,* the crisis is laid on his shoulders for action. This may be seen more clearly in an analysis of young Ged, the protagonist of the Earthsea Trilogy.

Le Guin introduces us to her subject immediately; the book is about Ged, called Duny as a boy and called Sparrowhawk familiarly, but it is about Ged the "dragonlord and Archmage." The story is thus of a young man learning about magic, and his place in relation to it. Certain stages in his sojourn to knowledge and mastery may be observed.

Naivete

The first stage in Ged's life is naivete. As goatherd in his native village of Ten Alders, Ged overhears his Aunt using a common, rustic spell on the animals. Ged duplicates the words, "not knowing their use or meaning or what kind of words they were" (p. 2). This spell, of course, works. The power is there; but Ged is an ingenue to this power. When the goats crowd around him he is terrified and unable to undo the spell. The significant thing here is that Ged is gifted with the innate ability to call upon the magical powers. As his Aunt observes: "He knew nothing, and yet had spellbound the goats to come to him and follow him, then she saw that he must have in him the makings of power" (p. 3). The gift is there, but it must be mastered. Magic does not belong to all men, but only to special, gifted men. Little is said in high fantasy about the origins of this gift. It seems, akin to Plato's "Myth of Er," an accident of birth. Possessing the gift, the youth must learn "the Balance and the Pattern which the true wizard knows and serves, and which keep him from using his spells unless real need demands" (p. 5).

This idea of the Balance or Pattern is central not only to Le Guin's portrayal of magic, but to much of her other fiction as well. In the *Earthsea Trilogy,* the Pattern derives from an eternal harmony of powers, also referred to by Le Guin as the Old Powers. These powers contain within them the possibility for good or evil use. It is man who upsets the pattern by his use of the powers. Thus the terrible danger of magic.

The Balance may be seen akin to the Buddhistic cosmology of harmonize tension in which all of one contrariety is interpenetrated by its reciprocal. Practically stated, every white contains a bit of black and *vice-versa*, every darkness contains a bit of light, every sorrow contains a bit of joy, and so forth. The aim of the Buddhistic follower is to so harmonize his own life by meditative processes as to attain an equilibrium between the tensions. The Buddha believed that the presence of evil is incontrovertible proof that there is no Creator, but simply the eternal existence of the aforesaid powers in tension. The adjective "eternal," however, must be qualified in that the Buddha also believed such a concept to be indeterminate. The task of man is the present attainment to peace and insight which individually restores a balance to the tension.

Perhaps because of the tidal sweep of Buddhism, and the renaissance of interest in its ancient texts in the 1960s and 70s in America, many readers of Le Guin have been a bit too quick to pigeonhole Le Guin into this philosophy. With some modification the sense of the Balance or Pattern is certainly allied with such a philosophy. By her own profession, Le Guin has admitted a far deeper influence from Jung. Some of this we have already observed in earlier chapters which considered her view of the effects of fantasy on the consciousness of man. The significance of the issue here resides in the ethical implications of actions. Having described herself once as a "congenital non-Christian," Le Guin has chosen to describe actions in specifically nontheological terms of "appropriateness." The application to the issue at hand may be observed in this statement of the author:

> Evil, then, appears in the fairy tale not as something diametrically opposed to good, but as inextricably involved with it, as in the yang-ying symbol. Neither is greater than the other, nor can human reason and virtue separate one from the other and choose between them. The hero or heroine is the one who sees the *whole*, which is greater than either evil or good. Their heroism is, in fact, their certainty. They do not act by rules; they simply know the way to go.[4]

Translated now, but rather circuitously, to the situation of Ged, we observe that the primary task for the Earthsea hero is to discern his own responsibility in relation to this whole, the Pattern. George Slusser is correct in his assertion that *"The Wizard of Earthsea*...explores in depth the question of individual responsibility."[5] In *The Farthest Shore,* the concluding volume of Le Guin's Trilogy, the narrator comments that:

> ...Mage and sailor are not so far apart; both not with the

powers of sky and sea, and bend great winds to the uses of their hands, bringing near what was remote. Archmage or Hawk the sea-trader, it came to much the same thing.[6]

Both mage and sailor interact with the powers they know, conscious that their actions involve others. The appropriate use of this power, which is ethical in its effect on others, is the question. This is also the question Ged would often in his human personality avoid:

'I do not want to go among men again tomorrow,' he said. 'I've been pretending that I am free.... That nothing's wrong in the world. That I'm not Archmage, not even sorcerer. That I'm Hawk of Temere, without responsibilities or privileges, owing nothing to anyone....' He stopped and after a while went on, 'Try to choose carefully, Arren, when the great choices must be made. When I was young, I had to choose between the life of being and the life of doing. And I leapt at the latter like a trout to a fly. But each deed you do, each act, binds you to itself and to its consequences, and makes you act again and yet again. Then very seldom do you come upon a space, a time like this, between act and act, when you may stop and simply be. Or wonder who, after all, you are.'[7]

Ged's ultimate responsibility is to come face to face with himself in the hazy realm of the Shadow; that nebulous interstice where the contrarieties (pride-humility, love-hatred) impinge upon each other and where a man's real self lies. Almost in Heraclitian language, Ged finds that wholeness resides in giving himself up. But before that final meeting at the conclusion of the book is engaged, Ged has considerable knowledge to acquire in the matter of his gift. For that we return to the second stage of his growth in magic.

Growing Awareness

Ged's original awareness of magic is simply an adolescent fascination with a foreign condition. It might equally have been a fascination for a budding Gontian maiden. Might have been; but with this exception. Fascination for the maiden would be common human instinct, fascination for magic is the response to a gift. One is response to an exterior presence; the other to an interior power. Still, it might have ended with little more than that—a goatherd casting minor spells—were it not for others who recognize the gifts in one "Mage born."

This in itself is another motif in fantasy magic. There are

others who are aware of the presence of this gift. It is never given nor exercised in solitude, and hence again we observe its ethical import. One finds a similar pattern in Susan Cooper's *Gray King* novels in which a kind of mystical bond identifies and locates the powers of the Old Ones. Similarly, Anne McCaffrey begins her *Dragonflight* novels with a search for the Weyrwoman, the gifted possessor of powers. Lessa, the object of the search in *Dragonflight,* is scarcely aware of her power, as is Ged at the beginning of the *Earthsea Trilogy*. Something is there; its precise nature and extent is only dimly guessed. And here is the danger. The possessor of the gift may think of himself as just that: a possessor. Rather, he is in the Balance a kind of curator.

As Ged becomes more aware of his innate power, he is reciprocated in his awareness by the appearance (or sending) of Ogion. Ogion appears in the literary fashion of the Mysterious Stranger: "So it happened that on the fifth day after the slaughter at Armouth a stranger came into Ten Alders village, a man neither young nor old, who came cloaked and bareheaded, lightly carrying a great staff of oak that was as tall as himself" (p. 13). In literary tradition this mysterious stranger, ambiguous and unusual, is a figure sent by spiritual powers or at the urging of such powers to tutor a hero into an awareness of the powers.

Ogion the Silent, Mage of Re Albi, initiates Ged into the second step of his magical awareness, an awareness acquired by knowledge of the powers and, in keeping with Le Guin's theme, knowledge of himself. The latter is signified by Duny's acquisition of his true name: Ged. The true name is a motif as common to world religions as it is to magic. The true name is more than an apellation; it is definition. In the Judeo-Christian tradition one finds an immediate example in Jehovah's naming of himself as the I Am That I Am in the theophany to Moses. The name was a definition of Jehovah as absolute authority, he need name himself by no other reference than himself and as absolute ontology, his being is complete himself. In fantasy, names similarly define the nature of the individual: "When you know the fourfoil in all its seasons root and leaf and flower, by sight and scent and seed, then you may learn its true name, knowing its being: which is more than its use" (p. 17).

A footnote must be added to Ged's case. Part of the effectiveness of fantasy literature surely lies in effective naming. In Le Guin's instance, the author will commonly listen to a kind of interior commentator, and allow that to select certain appropriate sound-names for her. With geographical place names she has on occasion been more whimsical, using names of her children, for example, for places in Earthsea. The point here is that Ged should most certainly not be construed as a play on God. In fact, when one critic suggested this to Le Guin, she was appropriately horrified. Ged is simply the defining, marking name reserved for the mage by the Old Powers.

 · With Ged thus designated by Ogion in a kind of baptism ritual, his training may go forward. The training under Ogion is at first rather startling in that nothing happens. Ogion instructs in silence. Nothing happens. No complicated charms, runes, or spells. Ged queries the method:

> 'When will my apprenticeship begin, Sir?'
> 'It has begun,' said Ogion.
> There was a silence, as if Ged was keeping back something he had to say. Then he said it: 'But I haven't learned anything yet!'
> 'Because you haven't found out what I am teaching,' replied the mage. (p. 17)

The problem for Ged is that "he hungered to learn, to gain power." But at this stage he wants power *for himself,* not to understand The Powers for their sake and for others.

For this, Ged receives further training at the School for Wizards.

Advanced Training

The School lies on the Isle of Roke, surrounded by the sea and a series of spells that retain order and balance. It is also a wizard's proving ground; one which not only instructs in the lore of wizardry that Ged has lusted for, but which instructs in that more indefinable lore of one's self. Already the Shadow is hounding Ged; and it is precisely that Jungian shadow of one's meeting with one's self. As it is in T.S. Eliot's poem *The Hollow Men,* the shadow represents the "bitter shock" of meeting one's own inner darkness. Between possibility and fulfillment, between idea and action, lies the shadow. In Eliot's phrasing:

> Between the idea
> And the reality
> Between the motion
> And the act
> Falls the Shadow[8]

Yet, this bitter shock is indispensable for spiritual or psychological rebirth. One must confront it. Jung said that "Everyone carries a shadow, and the less it is embodied in the individual's conscious life, the blacker and denser it is."[9] In Ged's situation, we might say that having been given his name he still must find the being thereby named, also the dangers, the darknesses attached to that being, and bring them to the foreground of conscious confrontation.

In addition, the meeting with the Shadow, again in Jungian terms, does not separate light and dark, new life and annihilation. It is conjunction. It is restoration of Balance through recognition and naming or identification. While Ged's training at Roke is apparently in magical knowledge, it is in reality a training in the meaning of the shadow. "The World is in balance, in Equilibrium," he is instructed, and this has implications for his wizardry:

> 'A wizard's power of Changing and of Summoning can shake the balance of the world. It is dangerous, that power. It is most perilous. It must follow knowledge, and serve need. To light a candle is to cast a shadow.' (p. 44)

The ever-present threat to the Balance is human pride, the will to bend the Balance to serve selfish ends. This is the danger always before Ged, and the danger that lies at the threshold of the Shadow:

> He did not see, or would not see, that in this rivalry, which he clung to and fostered as part of his own pride, there was anything of the danger, the darkness, of which the Master Hand had mildly warned him. (p. 45)

Ged's deadly rivalry with Jasper leads him to exercise power in an act of pride, and thereby the Shadow is loosed. Lord Gensher admonishes him:

> 'It has no name. You have great power inborn in you, and you used that power wrongly, to work a spell over which you had no control, not knowing how that spell affects the balance of light and dark, life and death, good and evil. And you were moved to do this by pride and by hate. Is it any wonder the result was ruin? You summoned a spirit from the dead, but with it came one of the Powers of unlife. Uncalled it came from a place where there are no names. Evil, it wills to work evil through you. The power you had to call it gives it power over you: you are connected. It is the shadow of your arrogance, the shadow of your ignorance, the shadow you cast. Has a shadow a name?' (p. 66)

The important passage affirms several things. Ged had power but not understanding. The power was exercised *for himself* and not for others. This fact constitutes the breaking of the Balance. The power thus unleashed is a power of evil, since anything contrary to the harmony of the Pattern is evil. Once summoned, evil has control over the summoner. The only possible resolution is for the summoner to control the evil, the shadow, by giving to it its true name. The rest of the book and indeed the entire trilogy in all its variegated action and incredible adventure is essentially the story of Ged's quest to subdue the Shadow and restore the Balance.

Mastery

In his acquisition of magical knowledge, Ged quickly outstrips even his masters at Roke. The preparation of his quest for the Shadow, however, is interior. There are certain constituents to his mastery of magic that accomplish his initiation and also assist his interior preparation.

First is simply the lore which the mage must achieve. He must know the true names of flora and fauna. No particle of life is too small to escape concern. Each contributes, part and parcel, to the Equilibrium. In addition he must master languages, and particularly the old speech of the Powers. Such language can provide communication even with dragons. Lastly, he must learn spells and charms which are considered tools, never ends in themselves. We have here, in a sense, the marriage of art and science that is akin to a medical surgery. The surgeon must master the tools, but to the ends of which his art guides him and the situation demands.

Secondly, and more importantly, is Ged's learning to act for and care for others. When confronting the dragon Yevaud, Ged learns that "It was not his own life that he bargained for." Something much larger; the whole archipelago that he had pledged himself to protect. This concern for others had also been reinforced by the ever-present pet, the Otak. The small beast and constant companion shows more than teaches Ged the art of compassion. After Ged has tracked a spirit to the deadlands, the Otak revives him by licking his parched forehead with its leathery tongue. The simple act of affection contained a profound lesson for Ged:

Later, when Ged thought back upon that night, he knew that had none touched him when he lay thus spirit-lost, had none called him back in some way, he might have been lost for good. It was only the dumb instinctive wisdom of the beast who licks his hurt companion to comfort him, and yet in that wisdom Ged saw something akin to his own power, something that went as deep as wizardry. From that time forth he believed that the wise man is one who never sets himself apart from other living things...." (p. 82).

In this act, Ged learns the *direction* his power must take; for others, not himself

Third, Ged learns to think of joy not in personal terms but in universal terms, particularly the restoration of the Pattern which his earlier greed had upset. These lessons collectively lead Ged to the conclusion that: "his task had never been to undo what he had done, but to finish what he had begun" (p. 148).

The mastery is not completed however, by knowledge, or concern for others, or a growing sense of universal order and joy in balance. It is completed in action. This is absolutely necessary in fantasy. No mental resolve in itself will conclude an issue. The action in this instance is Ged's confrontation with the Shadow, which is ultimately his final reconciliation with his own self and the subduing of the errors of pride. The quest leads over wild seas to a (magical) island of shifting sand. Onto that sand Ged strides. Upon that sand he confronts the many shapes that comprise the Shadow:

> At first it was shapeless, but as it drew nearer it took on the look of a man. An old man it seemed, grey and grim, coming towards Ged; but even as Ged saw his father the smith in that figure, he saw that it was not an old man but a young one. It was Jasper: Jasper's insolent handsome young face, and silver-clasped grey cloak, and stiff stride.... The look of Jasper fell from the figure that approached, and it became Pechvarry....(p. 178)

Why the shifting shapes? All these are part and parcel of Ged's nature. This he realizes as he names the Shadow: "Aloud and clearly, breaking that old silence, Ged spoke the shadow's name and in the same moment the shadow spoke without lips or tongue, saying the same word: 'Ged.' And the two voices were one voice" (p. 179).

In completion of this quest for wholeness, Estarriol, Ged's friend and in a sense our presence on the scene, reflects on the action: "He began to see the truth, that Ged had neither lost nor won but, naming the shadow of his death with his own name, had made himself whole: a man: who, knowing his whole true self, cannot be used or possessed by any power other than himself, and whose life therefore is lived for life's sake and never in the service of ruin, or pain, or hatred, or the dark" (p. 181-81).

It is clear, I believe, that even though Le Guin eschews traditional religious categories for action, the actions depicted in her works are decidedly moral, not just "appropriate." The good, in her view, consists of "wholeness," of recognition of one's self. But in that recognition there is also a clear sense that certain actions are evil, not just inappropriate, and that other actions are appropriate because they are good. Some of this may be semantic quarreling, but it deserves mention.

The certain thrust of Le Guin's use of magic in fantasy, however, cannot be denied. The possessor of the magical gift has the ability to wreak evil or to restore harmony. This is determined by actions. While Le Guin's presuppositions may differ from those of Lewis, her use of magic in relation to good and evil in the fiction provides an example of high fantasy at its best.

Chapter Six

The Quest

Ancient literatures and mythologies frequently based the action of a story upon a quest. In place of the quest, modern literature has often provided an adventure. The distinction lies at the heart of fantasy. If the fantasy hero must act, as we have observed earlier, he must often seek long and desperately for a basis for action. The question which this hero pursues is different from an adventure in several significant ways. In the first place, an adventure may lead anywhere. Jack Kerouac's *On The Road* is an adventure; the road takes the rider out, but the rider has no precise goal. The quest is always *toward* something, although that something often becomes clear only with the seeking of it. Second, the adventure may be undertaken for any number of reasons—boredom with one's present situation, a wanderlust, a dissatisfaction with things as they are. The quest, however, is always a spiritual or religious undertaking. The quest hero is appointed or ordained to his mission, and its end has spiritual signficance. Third, the adventure may be merely a whimsical frolic. In contrast, the quest is always a grave, serious undertaking. It is often life-threatening, marked by a sense of struggle, of imminent or immediate danger in which the character must call upon all of his will and power to push on.

The goal of fantasy, as we have observed, is to lead the reader to a keener understanding of himself and his world. Adventure often follows a path along which the reader may lose himself and his world. When Dylan Thomas wrote

> Twenty-four years remind the tears of my eyes.
> In the final direction of the elementary town
> I advance for as long as forever is

I suspect that through the verbal larding that fattens his work, Thomas was in search for that sacred altar of self-understanding. Recent biographies confirm my suspicion. Often in his turbulent, pub-crawling lifetime, Thomas retreated to the cottage at Blaen Cwm. The poems written there groped toward a way he would not go. When he described a saviour as "rarer than radium/commoner than water, crueller than truth," the saviour was nothing more than words full of pretty sounds. The Blaen Cwm, his writing haven, was *only* a hideaway. It was never a place from which he began anew. Fantasy provides not a hiding place but a point from which the reader can begin anew. The fantasy artist expects the reader to learn something about himself by having made a sojourn through fantasy. The writer invites the reader to probe his spiritual nature, to grow in experience, to resolve himself to new directions. The quest provides a basis for such exploration.

In a convincing essay W.H. Auden establishes the nature of the "true quest" in literary tradition. "To look for a lost button," argues Auden, "is not a true quest."[1] Why not? In the first place, because one knows precisely what he is looking for. Furthermore, the button is something once held in possession, and it can be regained in several ways. If one fails to find the button, a near duplicate may be purchased, or the coat from which it has been lost may be serviceable without the button, or the coat may be simply discarded. "To go in quest," Auden writes, "means to look for something of which one has, as yet, no experience; one can imagine what it will be like but whether one's picture is true or false will be known only when one has found it."[2]

The quest is one of the oldest literary forms. Greek heroic mythology is predicated upon its action. In fact, David Leeming notes in *Mythology: The Voyage of the Hero* that: "The quest myth in one sense is the *only* myth—that is, all other myths are a part of the quest myth. The hero's whole life from birth to apotheosis is a quest, whether for an actual place or object in this world, as is the case with Odysseus and Jason, or for eternal life in another world, as is the case with the great religious leaders such as Jesus and Quetzalcoatl."[3] Northrop Frye has similarly argued that "all literary genres are derived from the quest myth."[4] Surely the quest has had a profound impact upon modern literature. Byron used Manfred, Prometheus, and Childe Harold to exemplify his own tortured seeking. Browning gave us Roland winding his horn before a desolate tower. Camus' Sisyphus guides all of his work. Auden's achievement is to establish the following essential traits which unify the many variations of the quest from its earliest forms to its latest descendents:

1) A precious Object and/or Person to be found and possessed or married.
2) A long journey to find it, for its whereabouts are not originally known.
3) A hero. The precious Object cannot be found by anybody, but only by the one person who possesses the right qualities of breeding or character.
4) A Test or series of Tests by which the unworthy are screened out, and the hero revealed.
5) The Guardians of the Object who must be overcome before it can be won. They may be simply a further test of the hero's *arete,* or they may be malignant in themselves.
6) The Helpers who with their knowledge and magical powers assist the hero and but for whom he would never succeed. They may appear in human or in animal form.[5]

Auden's traits are an essential minimum for defining the quest. Although one particular trait may be given greater emphasis in any particular story, all must be present to some degree. However, Auden omits one essential trait which forms the background for any quest—a threat to the status quo. Quests are pursued only when grave events threaten the well-being of a society. This is true in ancient literature as well as modern fantasy. No quest is pursued for the sheer fun of it. The qualification is important since an adventure is often undertaken simply because the status quo has become torpid in its uneventfulness and the adventurer is motivated by little more than accentuated ennui. In the quest, the threat to the status quo often makes the hero long for the routine, and frequently the quest is pursued in order to recover that state.

It is true that what begins in adventure may end in a quest. Tolkien's *The Hobbit* appears at first to be adventure. Bilbo Baggins is disturbed from his routine by an unexpected visit and, as unexpectedly, finds himself on a voyage. Not until the graver implications of the arkenstone emerge, does the adventure become more universal in significance. Then Bilbo longs for the commonplace life of the shire, but he also realizes that such life cannot be regained without completing the quest. *The Hobbit* is rather unusual in its use of the quest, quite different for example, from *The Lord of the Rings* which begins in a situation of ominous events in which the threat is immediately present.

Richard Adams' fantasy *Watership Down* is a fine example of the quest motif in modern fantasy literature. The story begins with an immediate sense of unease, of the portent and threat which precipitate a quest. The pristine calm of the rabbit warren is suddenly disrupted one morning:

> A little way in front of them, the ground had been freshly
> disturbed. Two piles of earth lay on the grass. Heavy posts,
> reeking of creosote and paint, towered up as high as the holly
> trees in the hedge, and the board they carried threw a long
> shadow across the top of the field. Near one of the posts, a
> hammer and a few nails had been left behind.[6]

In reaction a rabbit character named Fiver immediately exclaims
to his friend, " 'Oh, Hazel! This is where it comes from! I know
now—something very bad! Some terrible thing—coming closer
and closer' " (p. 6).

The threat in this instance comes from the technological
instruments of man. In his rage for order and space, man is
bulldozing the warren. The workers have erected a sign whose
"hard letters...cut straight as black knives across its white
surface:"

> THIS IDEALLY SITUATED ESTATE, COMPRISING SIX ACRES
> OF EXCELLENT BUILDING LAND, IS TO BE DEVELOPED
> WITH HIGH CLASS MODERN RESIDENCES BY SUTCH AND
> MARTIN, LIMITED, OF NEWBURY, BERKS. (p. 7)

This one event is only a local manifestation, however, of a larger
evil in the world. It would be possible for the rabbits simply to
move on to a new warren. But how often can they move? What lies
behind this relentless desecration of the land? The physical
manifestation is only an adumbration of a dark shadow hovering
over the whole earth:

> 'Of course, I never sat down and thought,' said Fiver. "It would
> take the Threarah to think all that out. I simply had the screaming
> horrors. Great golden Frith, I hope I never have them like that again!
> I shall never forget it—that and the night I spent under the yew tree.
> There's terrible evil in the world."
> It comes from men,' said Holly. All other elil do what they have to
> do and Frith moves them as he moves us. They live on the earth and
> they need food. Men will never rest till they've spoiled the earth and
> destroyed the animals. (p. 136)

Hazel, the leader of the hares in the warren of Watership
Down, undertakes a long journey to resolve the threat. At the end
lies the most precious of all treasures to the hares: a home. The
goal is to restore the old order to the commonplace. Hazel is

acutely aware of this longing as the threat becomes more keen: "To come to the end of a time of anxiety and fear! To feel the cloud that hung over us lift and disperse—the cloud that dulled the heart and made happiness no more than a memory! This at least is one joy that must have been known by almost every living creature" (p. 51).

Hazel is indeed a hero on this quest for the precious object. He is not exceptionally strong nor uncommonly brave. But he is cunning, and he trusts wholly in the help of El-Ahrairah. Although he may often feel forsaken, Hazel always operates in an arena alive with spiritual presence. In *Symbolism and Belief,* Edwyn Bevan seems to refer to the heroic type represented by Hazel when he writes:

> To feel that the battle for good is ultimately a losing one in an indifferent universe may make your battle, if you persist, the more admirable, but the confidence that the battle will be victorious in the long run, that you are fighting with the universe on your side, or rather that you are fighting on the side of God, may give a spiritual quality to your fight even more admirable than heroic despair. After all there will still be opportunities for heroism enough, if you seek them, in standing against the evil which seems, by all the appearances of the hour, to tower triumphant.[7]

Hazel and the other hares have a keen sense of living a mythology, in a world alive with divine significance and direction. In fact, the direst threat of the machinations of man, we learn, is to this world.

The rabbits' mythology is structured in what one might call a harearchy of divinities. Frith is the supreme deity whose name means literally "The Lord Sun." In fact, Frith is the sun, which is regarded as a god by the rabbits. Frith is the giver of life, the ruler over order. Much more personable is the folk hero-deity El-Ahrairah, whose name translates as "Prince of a Thousand Enemies." If Frith is the transcendent God, El-Ahrairah is the immanent presence, the "God with us," and one might note that the prefix is adapted from the Hebrew word meaning "God." Both these deities, Frith and El-Ahrairah, are opposed to the Elil, the enemies of the rabbits who include the fox, the weasel, and man.

El-Ahrairah is the paradigm of the quest hero, the individual who relies on his own keen wit to overcome his thousand enemies. He is also, however, an omnipresent power who has left testament and pattern for others to follow. But it is still Hazel the individual who must undertake the long journey. He has El-Ahrairah as example, but he must act. Throughout the journey Hazel receives specific supernatural assistance from surprising creatures, but always the emphasis is upon individual action. Hazel confesses that all he can do is attempt the quest:

> "I don't know what I expected," said Hazel. "I'd never been near the Chief Rabbit before. But I thought, 'Well, even if he won't listen, at least no one can say afterward that we didn't do our best to warn him'." (p. 12-13)

By at least trying, by doing the best he is able under his own strength and the conditions of the moment, Hazel receives reciprocating help in several ways. One increasingly important source of strength is the premonitory gift of Fiver:

> 'There's a thick mist between the hills and us. I can't see through it, but through it we shall have to go. Or into it, anyway.'
> 'A mist?' said Hazel. 'What do you mean?'
> 'We're in for some mysterious trouble,' whispered Fiver, 'and it's not elil. It feels more like—like mist. Like being deceived and losing our way.' (p. 47)

Strange as Fiver's visions seem, Hazel respects them as a divine gift: " 'Never mind,' answered Hazel. 'We'll go down now. It's time we were getting them on again. If you have any more queer feelings like that, keep close to me. I'll look after you' " (p. 47). When Fiver's visions are ridiculed by others and even Hazel begins to doubt them, Fiver is emphatic in his faith in his visions: " '...It's simply that I *know* there's something unnatural and evil twisted all round this place. I don't know what it is, so no wonder I can't talk about it. I keep getting near it, though' " (p. 79).

A second form of supernatural aid to Hazel is directly from El-Ahrairah. Hazel's faith in the legendary hero is repeatedly tested, but each time the lesson of El-Ahrairah to individual cunning and wit is reaffirmed. In one legend of the rabbit mythology Frith is reported to encourage El-Ahairah thus:

> 'El-Ahrariah, your people cannot rule the world, for I will not have it so. All the world will be your enemy, Prince with a Thousand Enemies, and whenever they catch you, they will kill you. But first they must catch you, digger, listener, runner, prince with the swift warning. Be cunning and full of tricks and your people shall never be destroyed.' (p. 26)

The threat can be overcome.

Hazel and his band are keenly aware of living in a mythology. Their world has not been stripped spiritually bare by mechanical necessity. They are a folk with story, a sense of past purpose and place, and therefore also a folk with a sense of future. For someone whose future is open to him and whose future may be freely chosen, the quest is not only a real possibility, but a possibility of infinite worth. Auden points out that:

> Man is a history-making creature for whom the future is always open; human "nature" is a nature continually in quest of itself, obliged at every moment to transcend what it was a moment before. For man the present is not real but valuable. He can neither repeat the past exactly—every moment is unique—nor leave it behind—at every moment he adds to and thereby modifies all that has previously happened to him.[8]

Because of this sense of myth, the hares of Watership Down also have a sense of purpose and place in the midst of disorder. With the presence of a living past, they are not forsaken to a foreign world. In his discussion of the Romance tradition in *Love in the Western World,* Denis de Rougemont makes a point that is applicable to these questing hares. "A myth," writes de Rougemont, "makes it possible to become aware at a glance of certain types of *constant relations* and to disengage these from the welter of everyday appearances."[9] Moreover, de Rougemont adds, "a myth expresses the *rules of conduct* of a given social or religious group. It issues accordingly from whatever *sacred* principle has presided over the formation of this group."[10]

The "sacred principle," or directive and ordering power, in Adams' novel is revealed by the intercalary chapters which detail the "old stories." These stories appear at first as digressions or as mere page-filling entertainment. They are, however, the core of the fantasy, providing the spiritual arena for the whole quest. For example, the tales of El-Ahrairah's prowess and cunning are both a counterpart to Hazel's quest and they provide direction for Hazel. They bring a divine presence to bear upon his actions.

The tests which lie between Hazel and the treasure are awesome trials of his spiritual and physical resources. He is tried to the utmost, but at the end there is restoration:

> The warren prospered and so, in the fullness of time, did the new warren on the Belt, half Watership and half Efrafan—the warren that Hazel had first envisaged on that terrible evening when he set out alone to face General Woundwort and try to save his friends at all

odds. (pp. 425-25)

Moreover, following the conventional pattern of fantasy, this story ends in joy. Like Arthur being called to the Blessed Isle of Avilon, or Frodo being translated at the end of *The Lord of the Rings,* the heroic Hazel is called on:

> They went out past the young sentry, who paid the visitor no attention. The sun was shining and in spite of the cold there were a few bucks and does at stiffay, keeping out of the wind as they nibbled the shoots of spring grass. It seemed to Hazel that he would not be needing his body any more, so he left it lying on the edge of the ditch, but stopped for a moment to watch his rabbits and to try to get used to the extraordinary feeling that strength and speed were flowing inexhaustibly out of him into their sleek young bodies and healthy senses. (p. 426)

Hazel would concur with Tennyson's King Arthur, perhaps, who says, "The old order changeth, yielding place to new." Hazel's transition is a change from peace to peace, however, due to the accomplishment of his quest.

It has become fashionable in mainstream contemporary literature to have a character pursue a quest without finding any sure or certain answers, and thereby to posit that there is no clearly discernible answer available to man in this world. One may argue that this is not a quest at all in the true sense. Yet the Romantic legacy of unrequited longing has left its imprint on the modern mind. And the Victorian revolutionaries engraved it irrevocably. Robert Browning left us not only the portrait of Roland winding his horn before the deserted tower, but also these famous lines from "Andrea Del Sarto": "Ah, but a man's reach should exceed his grasp,/Or what's a heaven for?"

The revolutionary fervor of Victorian thinkers was accepted by twentieth-century existentialists as a cause in itself. Change, they cried, for the sake of change. Seek, for the sake of seeking.

This sense of ceaseless questing has pervaded modern existential literature. In his *Myth of Sisyphus*, Camus depicts the old hero ceaselessly striving to push his boulder heavenward. Camus comments: "The struggle itself toward the heights is enough to fill a man's heart. One must imagine Sisyphus happy."[11] Happiness lies in the seeking iself; not necessarily in the location of a goal. In effect, existential literature has ripped the heart out of Auden's scheme: the precious object to be discovered no longer exists.

One might argue that the precious object is man himself. That is a sound argument, and a pertinent one when one also accepts Lev Shestov's argument that "Necessity," the trait of our modern age in his view, denies man his own being.[12] In fantasy the precious object is finally a "regained clarity," to use Tolkien's term, of man himself in his present world. But fantasy insists that the quest does have a goal, that it does have direction, that the seeker is actively directed by divine, supernatural aids in locating that goal. The fantasy hero is not forsaken to a barren world of pointless seeking. In temperament modern existentialism is rooted in the Romantic revolution against established and unvarying order. Fantasy, as we have seen, shares some of that same Romantic soil for its literary goundwork, but it is a different flower in the garden. An interesting literary link, and one which is illuminating of the fantasy quest, may be found between the Romantic poet Novalis, the early fantasist George MacDonald, and C.S. Lewis.

Novalis, a self-confessed votary of the cult associated with the "Quest for the Blue Flower," a term that symbolizes an insatiable longing for an ideal which always seems just out of reach, was a powerful influence on George MacDonald. In fact, MacDonald wrote: "Shall I not one day, 'somewhere, somehow,' clasp the large hand of Novalis, and, gazing on his face, compare his features with those of Saint John?"[13] And in a preface to one of MacDonald's works, Lewis wrote that "Novalis is perhaps the greatest single influence on MacDonald—full of 'holiness,' gloriously German-romantic."[14] It is not unusual, perhaps, that the open-ended seeking of Novalis should influence the mystic sensibility of MacDonald. It is curious, however, that Lewis claimed MacDonald as his spiritual and literary mentor in much the same way that MacDonald did Novalis. Lewis wrote, for example, that what MacDonald's *Phantastes* "actually did to me was to convert, even to baptize...my imagination."[15]

MacDonald wrote *Phantastes* during two months of a particularly frenetic and critical year (1858) of his life. This work, more than any other, haunted Lewis's youth. *The Pilgrim's Regress* shows the direct result of this influence, specifically in development of this theme of unrequited longing, which Lewis calls *Sehnsucht* in deference to Novalis. In "The Fantastic Imagination in George MacDonald" Glenn Sadler points out several affinities between the two works:

> MacDonald's *Phantastes* is a poet's artistic diary of youthful dreams. Like Lewis's *Pilgrim Regress,* it is the record of a young man's spiritual contest with the "false objects" which taunt his thirst for the fulfillment of "Sweet Desire." Both Anodos and John search bravely for a realization in their actual life of dream-world aspirations. Both must forsake parental ties. Having strayed "far away from home John hears the plucking sound of the Aeolian harp beckoning him to " 'Come.' " Through a glassless window he sees, for the first time, the primrose woods of Desire....[16]

Reflecting at a later date on his first reading of *Phantastes,* Lewis recognized the dangers inherent in this romantic longing: "I had already been waist-deep in Romanticism; and likely enough, at any moment, to flounder into its darker and more evil forms, slithering down the steep descent that leads from the love of strangeness to that of eccentricity and thence to that of perversity."[17] Lewis, then, recognizes this longing and questing in his own personality and work, but also recognizes the danger of simply acting on this longing without any sense of direction. The distinction may be stated thus: romantic and existential seeking are often induced by a profound sense of alienation in this world and the effort somehow to appease one's own loneliness and longing. Thus, such seeking is inner-directed. The quest may originate from the same sense of alienation in this world, but its effort is somehow to rectify the situation in the world itself. The quest then is never individual, but social. One man may engage it; but he engages it for others.

In *Out of the Silent Planet* Lewis distinguishes between quests and individual longing by use of the terms *wondelone* and *hluntheline:* "These were two verbs which both, as far as he could see, meant to *long* or *yearn;* but the *hrossa* [creatures of the planet Mars] drew a sharp distinction, even an opposition, between them. Hyoi seemed to him merely to be saying that every one would long for it *(wondelone)* but no one in his senses could long for it *(hluntheline)*."[18] In this case *wondelone* is akin to the seeking of the quest, while *hluntheline* is conceived as the seeking of self-gratification. The distinction is further defined in this passage from *Perelandra:*

> As he let the empty gourd fall from his hand and was about to pluck a second one, it came into his head that he was now neither hungry nor thirsty. And yet to repeat a pleasure so intense and almost so spiritual seemed an obvious thing to do. His reason, or what we commonly take to be reason in our own world, was all in favour of tasting this miracle again; the childlike innocence of fruit, the labours he had undergone,

the uncertainty of the future, all seemed to commend the action. Yet something seemed opposed to this "reason." It is difficult to suppose that this opposition came from desire, for what desire would turn from so much deliciousness? But for whatever cause, it appeared to him better not to taste again. Perhaps the experience had been so complete that repetition would be a vulgarity—like asking to hear the same symphony twice in a day.[19]

Later Ransom, the space traveller and spiritual sojournor, reflects: "This itch to have things over again, as if life were a film that could be unrolled twice or even made to work backwards...was it possibly the root of all evil?"[20]

Perhaps not the root of all evil; but it certainly is the itch that motivates the self-appeasing seeking of many adventures. The quest is always toward final solution. Moreover, it is toward a joy which may transcend individual sacrifice in the sense that things are, by virtue of a completion of the quest, well with the world.

Fantasy literature is popularly construed as a light-hearted diversion from the tedium of modern life, a sound alternative, perhaps, to television. The genre is entertaining, marked by lively story, exciting events, and fascinating characters. It is possible, of course, to write bad fantasy, for as a literary genre it must first of all abide by aesthetic standards that will distinguish enduring significance in any literary work. Fantasy has no license to short-change the reader because it is unique.

But, assuming that the work meets the same criteria we invoke for excellence in any literary work, it seems to me that fantasy has an additional significance uniquely its own. It possesses, by virtue of the six traits we have examined, a certain gravity with which it addresses the spiritual issues of humankind. Fantasy may be light-hearted at times, but it is not to be taken lightly. The characters, be they human, animal, or alien, confront and work through problems common to man. Moreover, they arrive at solutions to those problems. These characters are tested in matters of good and evil in a way which defines their own heroism and provides us a standard by which to measure ours. They are not superstars. They are merely characters who endure, often in quiet and mild ways, in pursuit of a quest they believe is right and eminently worthwhile.

Finally, much of the appeal in modern fantasy resides in its optimism for humankind. The human spirit may be maligned, but it will endure. It may be tested, but it will be found worthy. In an age acutely pessimistic about the human race, fantasy remains adamant in its belief that man is worthy. There may be bad men among us—fantasy never denies this—but somehow even the feeblest of creatures can individually confront them. And fantasy believes the confrontation with evil in any of its multifaceted variations is worth the risk, the sorrow, the pain, for the struggle will come to an end, and at that end lies joy: "They both laughed. Laughed—the Mountains rang with it!"

Chapter Seven

A Contemporary Fantasy:
The Chronicles of Thomas Covenant,
Unbeliever

When J.R.R. Tolkien published *The Lord of the Rings* as a trilogy it was an accident born of expediency. Convinced that the book was too unwieldy and that twentieth-century readers simply could not be interested in a work whose length surpassed Dickensian dimensions, and convinced, furthermore, that interest in the work would wane even for those stalwart few who undertook its reading, publishers Allen and Unwin made a pragmatic decision to divide the work into three books and to reduce the print order on the second and third books.

A crucial little accident for contemporary fantasy. In the last decade several trilogies, an occasional tetralogy, and one or two pentalogies have appeared. Stephen R. Donaldson has spared us the linguistic crime of "hexalogy" by calling his fourth Thomas Covenant novel the first of the second trilogy.

To the delight of his readers, Donaldson has speculated nine Convenant novels, or three trilogies, a numerical significance which won't be lost on fantasy readers.

The sweep of the long or epic fantasy carries with it dangers and pleasures for both author and reader. The chief danger is that which dogged Charles Dickens every step of his novelistic way; that is, a tendency by the author to forget characters and events introduced in the early stages. A second, and more deadly danger is the failure to sustain pace and enthusiasm. The danger here is that the broad sweep produces heavy fluff. And the long fantasy can sometimes produce whole bushels. A word dropped careless on a page, observed Emily Dickinson, is a scar forever. The puffery of my pages may produce intolerable wounds.

But there are also pleasures in the epic span. If fantasy evokes another world, it takes time to get to know that world, to become familiar with its flowering. One admires and appreciates an able guide in a distant land. Furthermore, since fantasy deals in often terrible matters of good and evil, it is assuring to feel the author's sure and steady control over the conflict, to note ramifications and find resolution. While in commercial bookselling, publishers bend the knee before the avatar of *de gustibus non est disputandum,* fantasy does not purport to find the past merely "a bucket of ashes." While there is no disputing the matter of tastes, the diet may be nutritious. Fantasy is not a palliative served to the palates of intellectual aborigines.

It is no accident, then, that contemporary fantasies are often of great length, even stunning length in an age given to snap judgments in computer-like operations.

Among these lengthy works, *The Chronicles of Thomas Covenant, Unbeliever* is quite simply among the best both in conception and aesthetic richness. While Tolkien's great Trilogy stands as the literary pinnacle of his distinguished career, and was published when the author was 62, Donaldson's achievement has exploded on the literary world as the author's first work. *Lord Foul's Bane* appeared in 1977 near the time of the author's 30th birthday.[1]

Donaldson has drawn freely on his personal life experience to construct the world of *The Chronicles*, and the experiences mark the novel with a sure realism, a concreteness of place and person. This is seen most clearly in the protagonist and the setting of the Land. The protagonist, Thomas Covenant, has published a smashingly successful novel, and has relished the first fruits of public acclaim. We have an initial portrait of a man lionized by the public, a man others would see, would be close to. The relation is severed by the sudden appearance of Covenant's leprosy. The golden boy turns to lead. The hero is an outcast.

The encroachment of Covenant's dread disease is handled with sensitive but clincial skill. The reader is always aware of the "faint, sweet, sick smell of Covenant's infection," and is also aware of the personal devastation incurred by it. Fearful of having the disease transmitted to their son Roger, Covenant's wife Joan divorces him: "He had waved goodby to Joan with regret and quiet respect."[2] Beneath the panache of his ritualistically adopted order to check the disease, a cauldron of loneliness, fear, and rage boils in Covenant. To carry off even this complex introduction is a major work for the author. A protagonist who is an outcast, a tormented and terrorized man— terrorized by his own body; this is an unlikely hero. But it is a hero who accords with the commonality of the fantasy protagonist.

The sureness of handling this character certainly derives from Donaldson's early life in India where his father was a medical missionary and an orthopedic surgeon in a leprosarium. Donaldson observes of his father that "The rebuilding of hands and feet was work for an orthopedist, but he was involved not only in the medical but also the social and psychological dilemmas of the lepers."[3]

The same acute awareness of the "social and psychological dilemmas" of the leper Thomas Covenant is conveyed in *The Chronicles*. He is disclosed to us initially as being sucked into the maelstrom of his disease. We enter a leprosarium with Covenant where the tortured fellow sufferers of Hansen's disease create a surrealistic impression of abject horror. "Kill yourself," one patient rasps. "Better than this." But the struggle against the disease is precisely consonant to Covenant's struggle against the evil which Lord Foul has unleashed against the other world called the Land. In his primary world, Covenant decides to survive—only survive—despite the cross of social and psychological pain. There is an inversion in the fantasy world whereby his struggle to survive both helps and hinders him. To survive in the primary world he must, every moment, recognize that he is outcast, a leper, not a hero. In the fantasy world the very things that he cannot do in his primary world, he can do but should not. For example, in his primary world Covenant is sexually impotent. In the secondary world, believing he is impotent, he rapes the maiden Lena who has just saved him from great danger. The fruit of that act, both the deed itself and the daughter Elena produced by the act, will torment him throughout the tales. There exists, then, a terrible and ironic tension between the two worlds and also in Thomas Covenant who in the primary world is outcast and in the secondary world is called to be saviour. Covenant conceives of himself as only part of a man, and believes that "When inadequate men assumed huge burdens, the outcome could only serve Despite" (IW, 105). The irony is accentuated by the fact that his leprosy incurs the amputation of two fingers of his right hand, and thereby he appears in the fantasy world as a reincarnation of the legendary hero Berek Halfhand, a former savior of the Land.

This impossibly complex situation, full of irony and tension, is handled with grace and power by Donaldson. We are allowed so deeply into the mind of Thomas Covenant that we cross the boundary of worlds with absolute sureness. We are convinced, as is Covenant, that without action "the whole Land would become just another leper in Lord Foul's hands..." (IW, 106).

The passage, moreover, is made sure by the extension—again with tension and irony—of good and evil from our world to the secondary world and by the evocative, full description of that other world.

The evocation of the Land is one of the clearest portraits in fantasy literature. The Land is wounded, as is the protagonist, and seems a natural extension of his dilemma. But the Land is *a place,* a sure and certain place. In fact, it is a place very much like the India of Donaldson's youth. He has remarked this significance: " 'India is both a mysterious and exotic place...and a very grim place of human misery. I grew up with wild physical beauty, strange cultural evidence of magical or spiritual events. There was a snake charmer on every corner.' "[4] One might say, however, that India is a context for the Land, rather than the Land itself. This is a fantasy world so remarkably full and resplendent that the reader travels through it with increasing awareness and a sense of having been there before but of getting to know the place for the first time. Stylistically, Donaldson achieves a minor but important step by having Covenant called to this other world and appearing in it at the pinnacle of a mountain called Kevin's Watch. A guide is given to him, a mountain girl named Lena, who leads him, and the reader, *down* into the fantasy world with a sense of a certain guide.

This fantasy world is, moreover, a powerful study in good and evil. The land is torn apart by the demonic pride of Lord Foul who has broken into the Land to break it all to his authority. The Land was formed according to the laws of creation, and the laws are breaking to Foul's will. This is exemplified in part by his host of perverse and preternatural spawn called Demondim, strange aberrations of nature. Evil is a terribly potent force in these novels, and one feels the land itself trembling under its force. "Part of my conception of what evil is, is its capacity to believe in its own perfection," Donaldson has said.[5] Such is the case here. The terror of Lord Foul is his unmitigated reluctance to mediate. He must have *all* things under his authority. There is an either/or in *The Chronicles,* and the entire quest of Covenant is through the strong dialectic of its tension.

The terror in this series is the seeming helplessness of "the good" in contrast to the potency of Lord Foul. The good, after all, is bound to order, to law, and the opposing power deliberately works to destroy or subvert all law to pride, to its "perfection of power." In *The Power That Preserves,* Covenant says:

> Creators are the most helpless people alive. They have to work through unsufferable—they have to work through tools as blunt and misbegotten and useless as myself. Believe me, it's easier just to burn the world down, reduce it to innocent or clean or at least dead ash. (PTP, 130)

Ironcially, there is a Creator in this series, but he appears in Covenant's primary world as a beggar. He has power. He can offer Covenant gifts of healing or life in the Land. But he is also restricted by the very laws by which he has created. He cannot work against his own law of good. Thus he is the tragic god, the beggar of man to act according to the good he has been given.

The most potent instruments in the hands of Lord Foul to oppose this good are three demons called Ravers. These are described by Lord Mhoram in *The Illearth Wars:*

> They were triplets, the spawn of one birth from the womb of their long-forgotten mother, and their names were *samadhi, moksha,* and *turiya.* They hated the Earth and all its growing things, just as Lord Foul hates all life and love.... They have performed treachery for him when he could not show his hand, and have fought for him when he would not lead his armies. (TIW, 52)

There are other powers at Lord Foul's command. He uses, for example, the power of the earth through the Illearth Stone for his own end. And by that power he has created the thousands of deformed creatures, the ur-viles and cavewights, to serve in his vast armies.

Juxtaposed to these hideous forces are the remnants of the Creator's laws and the upholders of those laws. But they are a keen and loyal force, unbowed in their allegiance to the good and the belief that it must prevail. Officially the upholders of the law center in Revelstone, a marvelous structure carved by giants out of rock and pregnant with the earth's power. Here the political or spiritual heads, the Lords of the Land, meet in enclave, their power symbolized by the Staff of Law. But the power of good extends throughout the Land, to those who intuitively loathe the evil of Foul, to those who are given special gifts, to those who humbly pursue a course in life they believe is good because it does no one harm. And, most notably, Thomas Covenant, whose wild magic, symbolized by his wedding ring of white gold, is hardly understood by anyone, least of all Covenant himself.

The marvelous and ironic enigma of Covenant focuses the story. In their survey guide to fantasy literature entitled *Fantasy Literature,* authors Tymn, Zahorski, and Boyer describe Covenant thus: "This is not a Tolkien-like fantasy with a great hero eager to do service for a troubled land. Donaldson's antihero is a stubborn, unbelieving man whose first act in the Land is rape, and whose overall goal is self-preservation."[6] One takes exceptional liberty with literary tradition to call Covenant an anti-hero. It is not that he wills not to act, but that he is utterly baffled by the acts he commits and fearful of acts he might do. More properly, perhaps, we might call him simply a confused common man called to heroism that he does not fully understand, that is threatening to him, and that he rightly fears. Nonetheless, he does act. And in that action, which also accords with fantasy tradition, he is given notable helpers on his quest to restore the Land. These include a marvel of creatures common to the Land, those who will bear the full horror of the evil if it is not checked. And they include special helpers—the Bloodguard who provide physical protection, some magical helpers, the magnificent giant Foamfollower, the creation of whom constitutes one of the finest achievements in fantasy literature.

The narrative account of the *Chronicles* follows a two-fold plot similar to the dual worlds of the characters: Thomas Covenant's struggle to preserve himself against leprosy, and the stuggle to preserve the Land. Covenant is received in the Land as a hero, although he is ill-suited to heroism. The awe-inspiring reverence that many pay him lies ironically opposed to what the reader knows of Covenant. He cannot save himself; can he save others? He has all he can do to endure; can he somehow work in the Land so that it, and all its people, may endure? From the first moment on Kevin's Watch where Drool Rockworm manifests himself to Covenant in a demand for the Wild Magic of the white gold, the irony is never relaxed. The plot turns on this: the white gold may not be taken *from* Covenant, but it must be willingly given *by* him. Thus it is true, as Lord Mhoram states, that Covenant *is* the wild magic. His will is at stake. *Lord Foul's Bane* brings us to the point where Covenant discovers this at least:

> His heart beat out heavy jolts of fear. He cowered there on his knees, abandoned, bereft of eyes and light and mind by the extremity

of his dread, and his breath whimpered in this throat. But as the first rush of his panic passed, he recognized it. Fear—it was an emotion he understood, a part of the condition of his existence. And his heart went on beating. Lurching as if wounded, it still kept up his life.

Suddenly, convulsively, he raised his fists and struck at the shale on either side of his head, pounded to the rhythm of his pulse as if he were trying to beat rationality out of the dirt. No! No! I am going to *survive!*

The assertion steadied him. Survive! He was a leper, accustomed to fear. He knew how to deal with it. Discipline—discipline. (LFB, 437)

Subsequent Chronicles detail how Covenant transforms the power to merely survive to an active force which drives back the power of the Despiser. This willful change from inward to outward salvation removes him from the type of the anti-hero.

The Chronicles, however, are not simply stories of Thomas Covenant. The tapestry of these plots is so rich that it may be said that Covenant is the master thread which unifies them. The Land, its immense and effulgent beauty, its leaders and common people, forms the heart of the struggle. This is a land eminently worth fighting for, full of the magnificence and the treasure which stem from human hope.

The resolution of the conflict in *The Power that Preserves* is stunning. The Law of Death has been broken by Elena, daughter of Covenant's rape of Lena. Thus, indirectly, Covenant, who is destined to uphold the Law of Life, has been responsible for breaking the Law of Death. In the final confrontation at Foul's Creche, the dead Lords appear before Covenant and "In one voice like a thunder of abomination—one voice of outrage that shook Covenant to the marrow of his bones—they cried, 'Slay him! It is within your power. Do not heed his treacherous lies. In the name of all Earth and health, slay him!' " (TPP, 465). The will of the Land is bent to this plea, but Covenant realizes a larger thing than slaying; that is the terror of healing. He has within his power the diorthosis of the wounded land. Slaying is the way of Despite itself; healing the way of the created good. Moreover, in a kind of pathetic desperation Covenant acknowledges that this evil cannot be slain; it is always amid the affairs of men. Rather, the Law of the Good must be so potent as to overrule disorder with order: "In a voice thick with grief, he answered the Lords, 'I can't kill him. He always survives when you try to kill him. He comes back stronger than ever the next time. Despite is like that. I can't kill him!' " (TPP, 465).

Covenant counters the dismay of the Lords with a command

to laughter, for this uniquely human emotion of joy stands against all evil:

> 'Joy is in the ears that hear—remember? You told me that. I've got joy
> for you to hear. Listen to me. I've beaten the Despiser—this time. The
> Land is safe for now. I swear it. Now I want—Foamfollower!'
> Involuntary tears blurred his sight. 'I want you to laugh. Take joy in
> it. Bring some joy into this bloody hole. Laugh!' He swung back to
> shout at the Lords, 'Do you hear me? Let Foul alone! Heal yourselves!'
> (TPP, 466)

The laughter rings hollow at first, then wells in an ever-widening ocean of pure joy which smashes unrestrained against the halls of evil. Under the laughter evil itself, in the shape of Foul, shrinks, regresses:

> Lord Foul cringed at the sound. He strove to sustain his defiance,
> but could not. With a cry of mingled pain and fury, he covered his face
> and began to change. The years melted off his frame. His hair
> darkened, beard grew stiffer; with astonishing speed, he was
> becoming younger. And at the same time he lost solidity, stature. His
> body shrank and faded with every undone age. Soon he was a youth
> again, barely visible.
> Still the change did not stop. From a youth he became a child,
> growing steadily younger as he vanished. For an instant, he was a
> loud infant, squalling in his ancient frustration. Then he disappeared
> altogether. (TPP, 467)[7]

Certainly, joy itself will neither destroy nor chain the power of evil. This joy has arrived, in fantasy tradition, on the heels of long and terrible struggle. Nonetheless, it is the eucatastrophe which marks the transition of all great fantasy into joy.

But what joy for Covenant? There is always the transition to the world, where the everyday anguish of leprosy, of divorce, of being an outcast await him. In a dramatic scene the creator appears to Covenant in Covenant's world, again in the guise of the beggar we first met in *Lord Foul's Bane*. Covenant had freely responded to the Beggar's need: " 'Ah, but you were—free of my suasion, my power, my wish to make you my tool. Have I not said that the risk was great? Choiceless, you were given the power of choice. I elected you for the Land but did not compel you to serve my purpose in the Land. You were free to damn Land and Earth and Time and all, if you chose. Only through such a risk could I hope to preserve the rectitude of my creation!' " (TPP, 471-72). Now the beggar freely offers his power: " 'I wish to give you a gift—a guerdon to speak my wordless gratitude. Your world runs by Law, as does mine. And by any Law I am in your debt. You have retrieved my Earth from the brink of dissolution. I could give you precious gifts a dozen times over, and still not call the matter paid' " (TPP, 473). Immediately, Covenant begs the life of his friend in the Land, the giant Saltheart Foamfollower. This, however, is a gift not to be given since it counters the very law of the Land which Covenant has upheld. The beggar suggests an offer of Covenant's own life continued in the Land. The offer carries with it, of course, the laurels of honor, wealth, and, with the Land's healing influence, relief from disease. Instead, Covenant asks merely to survive, and the gift is granted:

> He was a sick man, a victim of Hansen's disease. But he was not a leper—not just a leper. He had the law of his illness carved in large, undeniable letters on the nerves of his body; but he was more than that. In the end, he had not failed the Land. And he had a heart which could still pump blood, bones which could still bear his weight; he had himself. (TPP, 480)

It would be derogating to *The Chronicles* to reduce them to plot synopses, but three items regarding the novelistic craft should be remarked in conclusion. The first is the evocative descriptive energy of the magical world. The power of magic is incremental through *The Chronicles,* gaining energy commensurately with Covenant's growing understanding of his own wild magic. In *Lord Foul's Bane,* the first novel, we are introduced to magic at the most elementary level. Lena, Covenant's guide, bathes his wounds with a healing mud called "hurtloam" and feeds him the aliantha berries which restore his strength. This is fundamental magic in fantasy and serves to introduce both Covenant and the reader to the nature of the Land. Gradually magic takes on more powerful dimensions with inventions such as earth power, the Staff of Law, the restorative powers of Lake Glimmermere, and Loric's Krill. Opposed to this is the increasing potency of Lord Foul's magic, from the perversion of life forms in cavewights and ur-viles to changes in the appearance of things in themselves and altering of nature itself. In a kind of Kantian reversal, we see the grotesque distortion of the phenomena, and wonder if the noumena are likewise breaking. Through this maze of distortion stands the deepening of Covenant's wild magic like a central director unifying musical antiphonies. At first his ring glows with a soft argent gleam. At times, without Covenant's full control, it flares into brutal and sudden power. By the third *Chronicle* the power is more decisively controlled and consequently focused and powerful. In the final confrontation with Lord Foul in *The Power that Preserves,* Donaldson fashions this moving scene of magical powers:

> Again Lord Foul struck. Power that fried the air between them sprang at Covenant, strove to interrupt the white, windless gale of the ring. Their conflict coruscated through the thronehall like a mad gibberish of lightning, green and white blasting, battering, devouring each other like all the storms of the world gone insane. (PTP, 462)

Realizing better than anyone in the Land the true nature of Foul, by his recognition that "Lord Foul was only an externalized part of himself," that each man bears within himself the possibility of evil, Covenant bends all his leper's will against that evil:

> Lord Foul's aura resisted with shrieks and showers of sparks. It was tough, obdurate; it shed Covenant's feral bolts as if they were mere show, incandescent child's play. But he refused to be denied. The dazzling of his wild magic flung shafts and quarrels of might at the emerald glister of the aura until one prodigious blast pierced it.
> It ruptured with a shock which jarred the thronehall like an earth tremor. Waves of concussion pealed at Covenant's head, hammered at his sore and feverish skull. But he clung to his power, did not let his will wince.
> The whole penumbra burst into flame like a skin of green tinder, and as it burned it tore, peeled away, fell in hot shreds and tatters to the floor. (PTP, 463)

The vigor of the language here evidences not only Covenant's wild magic in full power, but the complete transformation of the potential anti-hero into the hero risking himself for the Land.

In the first volume of the second trilogy, *The Wounded Land,* Covenant's power flares more freely, almost as if having unlocked the power he is losing control of it. The power appears suddenly and explosively, triggered by something beyond his will:

> Before Sivit could strike, white flame exploded around Covenant, enveloping him in conflagration. He burned with silver fury, curuscated the air. Linden recoiled, flung up her hands to ward her face. Wild magic began to erupt in all directions.
> A rampage of force tore Sivit's scepter from his hands. The iron fired black, red, white, then melted into slag on the ground. Argent lashed the bonfire; flaming brands scattered across the circle. Wild

lightning sizzled into the heavens until the sky screamed and the crystal walls rang out celestial peals of power. (TWL, 193)

The key word in the foregoing passage is "erupts." Again and again the wild magic explodes of its own accord. The issue becomes this: once given power, can Covenant control it, or will he be destroyed by it? One remembers the High Lord's words: "You are the wild magic." Perhaps the final act of heroism in fantasy literature is the hero's control over his own heroism.

A second item to be remarked here is Donaldson's linguistic ability to convey such portrayals of power. The entire work is a symphony of vivid linguistic skill approaching crescendos in the manifestations of power. The work is marked by fluidity and grace throughout. One senses this first in Donaldson's skill at naming, an "elvish" talent he shares with Tolkien. The names of characters and places are apt and often archetypal. For example, the names of Lord Foul's three demons are resonant of Hebrew malediction. The Illearth stone, Lord Foul's source of power, is in fact ill earth. A number of portmanteau words such as Hearthrall and Hearthew are used, along with evocative sound names. The significance of names in fantasy literature should not be underestimated. They should be both alien and familiar. Too often modern fantasy has shown a perverse tendency only to the former with heiroglyphic names that signify only a cipher. With such the reader remains a stranger in a strange land. Donaldson's names hold and home us with familiarity on distant shores.

The linguistic ease displayed in naming is also evident in the ease of the prose line. The prose has a tougher, tauter pace than the poetic flights of Lord Dunsany, for example. But this is rich and compelling prose of the first order, even lush at times. The sentences are marked by vigorous verbs, powerful rhythms, and variations of form to the tale and emotion. Donaldson does have a tendency to be arcane in his diction. The reader will find many unfamiliar words here, which is an unusual characteristic of the genre. At times it almost seems the dictionary is opened to a certain section and one finds a string of words such as *condign, condignity, cerements, ceremental, caducity, crepuscular,* and *chrism* in short order. By contrast, Tolkien, master of languages, wrote with a very subdued, even vocabulary. Donaldson often delights in the unusual, particularly the Latinate word, but it is always used with precision and power. In sum the linguistic skills provide the work with an aesthetic richness that rank the work among the best in the genre.

This third particular trait of consideration here is the ease of transference between worlds. A organic part of the plot, the transference between the two worlds is executed with remarkable ease and unity. Covenant's leprosy is a central issue in the Land as it is in the World. His love for his divorced wife Joan is equally apparent in each world. The transference is strengthened in *The Illearth War* by the appearance of another Worldling, Hile Troy, in the Land. Troy, a blind military genius, plays a strategic if enigmatic role in the battles to preserve the Land. A richer character than Troy is Dr. Linden Avery of *The Wounded Land,* first volume of the second trilogy. A stunningly complex woman, she brings a whole new dimension to the Land by her trained scientific procedure and her willful unbelief in evil. The distinction from Covenant's unbelief is clear. Covenant forced himself, at first, to unbelief in the land since survival as a leper meant willful and rigorous concentration on the fact of the disease every moment. Thus a land which acts as a restorative and healing agent must be a dangerous and tempting illusion. Survival in his world demands unbelief in the Land. His growing belief in the Land, however, is caused by his unavoidable recognition of the presence of evil in that land. That evil is real, and deadly potent. Dr. Avery's unbelief has to do with the nature of evil itself. In her clinical world evil is a popular and unlearned name for disease. Her careful fabric of unbelief begins to unravel in this world:

> What had happened to her? She understood nothing about evil, did not even believe in it as an idea; but she had seen it in Joan's feral hunger. She was trained to perceive the world in terms of dysfunction and disease, medication and treatment, success or death. Words like *good* or *evil* meant nothing to her. (TWL, 30)

Dr. Avery refuses to believe in Joan's possession, nor does she believe in a land possessed by the evil of Lord Foul. The skeptic in an alien land. We have in Dr. Linden Avery the supreme achievement of fantasy; probing, questioning, and slowly subjected to our belief. She is there to question for us this reality. When Covenant lies wounded, she reflects that "This sickness was a moral evil" (TWL, 200). Slowly, terribly, she is baptized in the hope that the land is real, and, perhaps, may be saved. Hers is a corrosive journey toward such hope, and by the end of the novel the hope is badly frayed, but endures.

The Chronicles of Thomas Covenant, Unbeliever forge a powerful link in the literary chain of fantasy tradition. Donaldson has given us a protagonist of huge pathos and unmitigated nobility. The tales, for all their prolific expanse, are webbed tightly by a stylistic skill rare in our time. The final end is to see our world more clearly, if not for the first time.

Notes

Chapter One: Introduction

[1]J.R.R. Tolkien, "On Fairy-Stories," *The Tolkien Reader* (New York: Ballantine, 1966), p. 39.

[2]Bruno Bettelheim, *The Uses of Enchantment: The Meaning and Importance of Fairy Tales* (New York: Vintage, 1977), p. 3.

[3]Recent sales figures are becoming increasingly difficult to obtain as more publishers are swallowed by conglomerates. In 1978, however, Ballantine projected sales of 850,000 copies for Tolkien's *Silmarillion,* a work which the author began as early as 1917, abandoned early in his career as unsatisfactory, attempted to revise and complete before his death, and which was finally completed by his son Christopher. Richard Adams' *Watership Down* was expected to sell 125,000 copies during its fourth year in print. The perennial *Winnie-The-Pooh* moved over 100,000 copies into young and eager hands. In one month an "epic" fantasy by Terry Brooks, *The Sword of Shannara,* sold 125,000 copies. The list may be continued into the satellite propositions such as the Brothers Hildebrandt Tolkien Calendar which sold a half million copies in 1977. It is good to remember, however, that numbers alone, while impressive, are relatively meaningless. One recalls that Raynor Unwin (of George Allen & Unwin, Tolkien's British Publisher) expected to lose 1,000 pounds on the first edition of the *Fellowship of the Ring* on an initial printing of only 10,000 total copies of the trilogy. One has to look well past the numbers and popularity to assess the significance and meaning of fantasy literature.

[4]The leading organization for scholarly interchange, The Modern Language Association, hosted a Conference on Science Fiction at its 1958 New York Convention. Now the Seminar on Science Fiction, it has met annually since 1958 and has come to pay closer attention to fantasy literature. The journal *Extrapolation,* first published in December, 1959, was founded as a Newsletter to print proceedings and papers of the Seminar.

[5]Ursula K. Le Guin, "From Elfland to Poughkeepsie," *The Language of the Night,* ed. Susan Wood (New York: G.P. Putnam's Sons, 1979), p. 93.

[6]C.S. Lewis, *A Preface to Paradise Lost* (New York: Oxford University Press, 1961), p. 1.

[7]Ibid., p. 3.

[8]*John Gardner, Grendel* (New York: Ballantine Books, 1970), p. 121.

Chapter Two: Story

[1]C.S. Lewis, "Sometimes Fairy Stories May Say Best What's to be Said," *Of Other Worlds,* ed. Walter Hooper (London, Bles, 1966), p. 36.

[2]C. Hugh Holman, *A Handbook to Literature*, 3rd ed. (New York: Odyssey, 1972), p. 13.

[3]Peter J. Schakel, *Reading with the Heart: The Way into Narnia* (Grand Rapids, MI: Eerdmans, 1979).

[4]Ursula K. Le Guin, "Dreams Must Explain Themselves," *Language of the Night,* p. 53.

[5]J.R.R. Tolkien, "Foreword," *The Fellowship of the Ring* (New York: Ballantine, 1965), p. xi.

⁶Ibid., p. ix.

⁷William Ready, *Understanding Tolkien and "The Lord of the Rings"* (New York: Warner Paperbacks, 1969), p. 34.

⁸C.S. Lewis, *Letters of C.S. Lewis,* ed. W.H. Lewis (New York: Harcourt, Brace & World, 1966), p. 271.

⁹*Ibid.*

¹⁰C.S. Lewis, "The Gods Return to Earth," *Time and Tide,* 34 (August 14, 1954), 1082.

¹¹J.R.R. Tolkien, *The Hobbit* (New York: Ballantine, 1966), p. 70.

¹²J.R.R. Tolkien, "Leaf by Niggle," *The Tolkien Reader* (New York: Ballantine, 1966), p. 101.

¹³Sam J. Lundwall, *Science Fiction: An Illustrated History* (New York: Grosset & Dunlap, 1978), p. 9.

¹⁴Ibid.

¹⁵Darko Suvin, "On the Poetics of the Science Fiction Genre," *College English,* 34 (December, 1972), 372-83.

¹⁶Ben Bova, "The Role of Science Fiction," *Science Fiction: Today and Tomorrow,* ed. Reginald Bretnor (New York: Harper and Row, 1974), p. 14.

¹⁷Lundwall, *Science Fiction: An Illustrated History,* p. 11.

¹⁸Ben Bova, "The Role of Science Fiction," p. 4.

¹⁹Mark Rose, "Introduction," *Science Fiction: A Collection of Critical Essays,* ed. Mark Rose (Englewood Cliffs, NJ: Prentice-Hall, Inc., 1976), p. 6.

²⁰C.N. Manlove, *Modern Fantasy: Five Studies* (Cambridge: Cambridge University Press, 1975).

²¹Aldous Huxley, *Brave New World* (New York: Harper and Row, 1946), p. 163.

²²W. Andrew Hoffecker, "A Reading of *Brave New World*: Dystopianism in Historical Perspective," *Christianity and Literature,* v. 29, #2 (Winter, 1980), p. 46.

²³Ibid., p. 49.

²⁴Arthur C. Clarke, *Childhood's End* (New York: Ballantine, 1953), p. 16. All quotations from *Childhood's End* are from this edition and page numbers will be entered parenthetically hereafter.

²⁵Walter M. Miller, Jr., *A Canticle for Leibowitz* (New York: Bantam Books, 1961), pp. 51-52. All quotations from *A Canticle* are from this edition and page numbers will be entered parenthetically hereafter.

²⁶From an Interim Lecture entitled "By Faith, Fantasy," delivered at Calvin College, Grand Rapids, Michigan, January 21, 1981.

²⁷Charles Moorman, *Arthurian Triptych: Mythic Materials in Charles Williams, C.S. Lewis, and T.S. Eliot* (Berkeley: University of California Press, 1960), p. 2.

²⁸The latter term, mythos, is perhaps most confusing, since it is rather recent to contemporary critical usage. Often the term, which is derived from the Greek root for "story", means in modern critical usage a world and life view revealed by the author or narrator of the story. "Mythopoeic" has a very specific etymology from the Greek *mythopoiia* which is the making of myths or fables. The term refers specifically to the narrative structure of the work; that is, rather than narrating an event that could *possibly* happen given certain characteristics of the narrative world. "Mythology" is usually limited to the inheritance of ancient literatures (which were often mythopoeic).

²⁹Mircea Eliade, *Myth and Reality,* trans. Willard R. Trask (New York: Harper & Row, 1963), p. 1.

³⁰Ibid., pp. 1-2.

³¹Ursula K. Le Guin, "Myth and Archetype in Science Fiction," *Language of the Night,* p. 78.

³²Frank Herbert, *Dune Messiah* (New York: G.P. Putnam's Sons, 1969), p. 188.

[33]Ibid., p. 193.

[34]Joseph Campbell, with whose views on myth I am in essential disagreement, is far more emphatic on this point. He states that "With our old mythologically bounded taboos unsettled by our own modern sciences, there is everywhere in the civilized world a rapidly rising incidence of vice and crime, mental disorders, suicides and dope addictions, shattered homes, impudent children, violence, murder, and despair" *Myths to Live By* (New York: Viking Press, 1972). My disagreement with Campbell centers on his argument that this state of contemporary affairs warrants the absolute forsaking of myth in the traditional sense in favor of total concentration upon the technological spirit of our age.

[35]C.S. Lewis, *The Abolition of Man* (New York: Macmillan, 1947), p. 71.

[36]Eliade, *Myth and Reality*, pp. 5-6. In her fine study of T.S. Eliot, Elizabeth Drew devotes a revealing chapter to Eliot's use of myth. There Drew argues that "Myth (the etymological root is the same as that of *mystery*) leads us back to ultimate mysteries, not only the mystery of life itself, but of that element in life by which man differentiated himself from the rest of the animal creation: speech," *T.S. Eliot: The Design of His Poetry* (New York: Charles Scribner's Sons, 1949), p. 2. Drew concludes that "The mythical method is the presentation of experience in symbolic form, the earliest and still the most direct and immediate form of human expression" (p. 3). Myth, then, may be considered the mode of revealing a spiritual insight through words, but seeks an immediate apprehension of spiritual truths which lie beyond words.

[37]Ibid., p. 34.

[38]Maud Bodkin, *Archetypal Patterns in Poetry* (London: Oxford University Press, 1934), p. 4.

[39]Northrop Frye, *Anatomy of Criticism* (Princeton: Princeton University Press, 1957).

[40]Le Guin, "The Child and the Shadow," *Language of the Night,* p. 62.

[41]Additional works helpful to an understanding of archetypes are: John J. White, *Mythology in the Modern Novel* (Princeton: Princeton University Press, 1971), and chapter four of *A Handbook of Critical Approaches to Literature* by Guerin, *et. al.* (New York: Harper & Row, 1966).

[42]Eliade, *Myth and Reality,* p. 81.

[43]J.R.R. Tolkien, *The Hobbit* (New York: Ballantine, 1966), p. 205.

Chapter Three

[1]C.S. Lewis, *The Pilgrim's Regress* (Grand Rapids: Eerdmans, 1958), p. 5.

[2]Bruno Bettelheim provides psychological analysis of bowdlerization of fairy stories in *The Uses of Enchantment.* See, for example his discussion of "Goldilocks and the Three Bears."

[3]Charles Muscatine, "The Nun's Priest's Tale," *Discussions of the Canterbury Tales,* ed. Charles Owen, Jr. (Boston: D.C. Heath, 1961), p. 59.

[4]Walter Wangerin, Jr., *The Book of the Dun Cow* (New York: Harper & Row, 1978).

[5]Harold Bloom, *Blake's Apocalypse: A Study in Poetic Argument* (Garden City, NY: Doubleday, 1963), p. 46.

[6]Friedrich Schiller, *Naive and Sentimental Poetry,* in the companion volume with *On The Sublime,* trans. Julius A. Elias (New York: Frederick Ungar, 1966), p. 85.

[7]Ibid., p. 87.

[8]Ursula K. Le Guin, "This Fear of Dragons," *The Thorny Paradise,* ed. Edward Blicken (Middlesex: Bles, 1975), p. 91.

⁹Charles Dickens, *Bleak House* (Boston: Riverside, 1956), p. 11.

¹⁰Charles Dickens, *Dombey and Son* (New York: New American Library, 1964), p. 157.

¹¹Thomas Hardy, *Jude the Obscure* (Boston: Houghton Mifflin, 1965), p. 17.

¹²Madeleine L'Engle, *A Wrinkle in Time* (New York: Dell Publishing Company, 1962), p. 4.

¹³Robert Siegel, *Alpha Centauri* (Westchester, Il: Cornerstone Books, 1980), p. 12.

¹⁴C.S. Lewis, "On Stories," *Of Other Worlds,* ed. Walter Hooper (New York: Harcourt, Brace & World, 1966), p. 15.

¹⁵C.J. Jung, *The Development of Personality, Collected Works,* Vol. 17 (New York: Pantheon Books, 1954), p. 170.

¹⁶C.S. Lewis, *An Experiment in Criticism* (Cambridge: Cambridge University Press, 1961), p. 72.

¹⁷C.S. Lewis, *The Magician's Nephew* (New York: Macmillan, 1970), p. 18.

¹⁸Thomas Greene, *The Descent from Heaven: A Study in Epic Continuity* (New Haven: Yale University Press, 1963), p. 15.

¹⁹George Edgar Slusser, *The Farthest Shores of Ursula K. Le Guin* (San Bernardino: Borgo Press, 1976), p. 35.

²⁰Victor Brombert, *The Intellectual Hero: Studies in the French Novel 1880-1955* (New York: J.B. Lippincott, 1961), p. 194.

²¹Ibid., pp. 194-95.

Chapter Four

¹Eric S. Rabkin, *The Fantastic in Literature* (Princeton: Princeton University Press, 1976), p. 28.

²Ibid., p. 4.

³C.N. Manlove, *Modern Fantasy: Five Studies* (Cambridge: Cambridge University Press, 1976), p. 28.

⁴Robert Scholes, "Science Fiction as Conscience," *The New Republic,* 175 (October 30, 1976), p. 40.

⁵Rabkin, *The Fantastic in Literature,* p. 45.

⁶Ursula K. Le Guin, *The Dispossessed* (New York: Avon, 1975), p. 68.

⁷Antoine de Saint Exupery, *The Little Prince,* trans. Katherine Woods (New York: Harcourt, Brace & World, 1971).

⁸J.R.R. Tolkien, "On Fairy Stories," *The Tolkien Reader* (New York: Ballantine, 1966), p. 46. All quotations from "On Fairy Stories" are from this edition, and hereafter page numbers will be entered parenthetically.

⁹J.R.R. Tolkien, *The Hobbit* (New York: Ballantine, 1966), p. 15.

¹⁰Ibid., p. 16.

¹¹Ibid., p. 17.

¹²Richard Adams, *Watership Down* (New York: Macmillan, 1972), p. 3.

¹³Peter S. Beagle, *The Last Unicorn* (New York: Ballantine, 1968), p. 1.

¹⁴William Ready, *Understanding Tolkien and the Lord of the Rings* (New York: Warner, 1968), p. 57.

¹⁵Eric S. Rabkin, ed., "Introduction," *Fantastic Worlds: Myths, Tales, and Stories* (New York: Oxford University Press, 1979), p. 3.

¹⁶Ibid.

¹⁷Ibid., p.4.

¹⁸J.R.R. Tolkien *The Return of the King* (New York: Ballantine, 1965), p. 370.

¹⁹Harvey Cox, *The Feast of Fools: A Theological Essay on Festivity and Fantasy* (Cambridge: Harvard University Press, 1969), p. 7.

²⁰Ibid., p. 59.

[21]Friedrich Heer, *The Medieval World,* trans. Janet Sondheimer (New York: New American Library, 1961), p. 168.

[22]Particularly valuable to literary historians is Christopher Ricks' edition of Tennyson's *Idylls* in which the variorum comparisons to the *Mabinogion* are amply set forth.

[23]Sir Henry Holland, "The Progress and Spirit of Physical Science," *Edinburgh Review,* 108 (1858), p. 71.

[24]Walter E. Houghton, *The Victorian Frame of Mind* (New Haven: Yale University Press, 1957), p. 1.

[25]Joanna Richardson, *The Pre-Eminent Victorian* (London: Jonathan Cape, 1962), p. 114.

[26]Tennyson, *The Poems of Tennyson,* ed. Christopher Ricks (London: Longmans, 1969), p. 1462. Hallam concedes, however, that the production of the *Idylls* was not as linear as this quotation suggests. In fact, Tennyson was continually revising and recasting individual *Idylls* as well as the work as a whole. In his *Tennyson* (New York: Collier, 1972), Ricks reports that in 1858 Tennyson wrote to his American publisher:

> I wish that you would disabuse your own minds and those of others, as far as you can, of the fancy that I am about an Epic of king Arthur.
>   I should be crazed to attempt such a thing in the heart of the 19th Century. (p. 264)

[27]Ibid., p. 1463.

[28]Ibid., p. 1464.

[29]Clyde de L. Ryals, *From the Great Deep* (Athens: Ohio University Press, 1967), p. 6.

[30]All quotations from *The Idylls* are from the Christopher Ricks edition, *The Poems of Tennyson* (London: Longmans, 1969), and will be identified by the title of the individual Idyll.

[31]I believe Tennyson would have agreed with Harvard law professor Lawrence Tribe in his essay in the July, 1979 *Atlantic* calling for selective deregulation of American society. The overwhelming impact of the argument lies in Tribe's marshalling of statistics that indicate precisely how legalized our society has become. Tribe observes: "Clearly, something is awry. For too long we have reflexively relied on law to right every wrong. We think of the rule of law, justice under law, peace through law—as though law and the legal process were perfectly synonymous with fairness and equity."

[32]Charles Williams, *Taliessin Through Logres* (Grand Rapids: Eerdmans, 1974), p. 19.

Chapter Five

[1]Brian Attebery, *The Fantasy Tradition in American Literature* (Bloomington: Indiana University Press, 1980), p. 13.

[2]Ursula K. Le Guin, *A Wizard of Earthsea,* (New York: Bantam Books, 1975), p. 23. All quotations from *A Wizard of Earthsea* are from this edition and hereafter page numbers of quotations will be entered parenthetically in the text.

[3]C.S. Lewis, *The Magician's Nephew* (New York: Macmillan, 1970), p. 72. All quotations from *The Magician's Nephew* are from this edition and hereafter page numbers of quotations will be entered parenthetically in the text.

[4]Le Guin, "The Child and the Shadow," *Language of the Night* ed. Susan Wood (New York: G.P. Putnam's Sons, 1979), pp. 66-67.

[5]George Edgar Slusser, *The Farthest Shores of Ursula K. Le Guin* (San Bernardino: Borgo Press, 1976), p. 35.

[6]Le Guin, *The Farthest Shore* (New York: Bantam, 1975), p. 34.

[7]Ibid.

[8]T.S. Eliot, "The Hollow Men," *The Complete Poems and Plays of T.S. Eliot* (New York: Harcourt, Brace & World, 1952), p. 58.

[9]Carl Justav Jung, *Psychology and Religion: West and East,* Bollingen Series XX, *The Collected Works of C.G. Jung,* vol. 11 (New York: Pantheon Books, 1958), p. 76.

Chapter Six

[1]W.H. Auden, "The Quest Hero," *The Texas Quarterly,* Vol. 9 (1962), pp. 81-93. Rprt. in *Tolkien and the Critics*, ed. Neil D. Isaacs and Rose A. Zimbardo (Notre Dame: University of Notre Dame Press, 1968), p. 40. Page numbers in following notes refer to the latter edition.

[2]Ibid.

[3]David Adams Leeming, *Mythology: The Voyage of the Hero* (New York: J.B. Lippincott, 1973), p. 184.

[4]Northrop Frye, *Fables of Identity: Studies in Poetic Mythology* (New York: Harbinger Books, 1963), p. 17.

[5]Auden, p. 44.

[6]Richard Adams, *Watership Down* (New York: Macmillan, 1972), p. 6. All quotations from *Watership Down* are from this edition and page numbers will be entered parenthetically hereafter.

[7]Edwyn Bevan, *Symbolism and Belief* (London: George Allen & Unwin, 1938), p. 377.

[8]Auden, p. 40.

[9]Denis de Rougemont, *Love in the Western World* (New York: Fawcett, 1956), p. 18.

[10]Ibid., pp. 18-19.

[11]Albert Camus, *The Myth of Sisyphus and Other Essays*, trans. Justin O'Brien (New York: Vintage Books, 1955), p. 91.

[12]See, for example, Lev Shestov, *Athens and Jerusalem,* trans. Bernard Martin (New York: Simon and Schuster, 1966). Here Shestov argues that "the task of philosophy consists in teaching men to submit joyously to Necessity which hears nothing and is indifferent to all" (p. 80).

[13]George MacDonald, "Essays on Some of the Forms of Literature," *A Dish of Orts* (London: 1893), p. 230.

[14]This quotation from Lewis on Novalis is from an unpublished letter dated 13 August 1930 and is quoted by Glenn Edward Sadler in "Fantastic Imagination in MacDonald," *Imagination and the Spirit.* (Grand Rapids: Eerdmans, 1971).

[15]C.S. Lewis, "Preface," *George MacDonald: An Anthology* (New York: Macmillan, 1947), p. xxxiii.

[16]Glenn Edward Sadler, "The Fantastic Imagination in George MacDonald," *Imagination and the Spirit* (Grand Rapids: Eerdmans, 1971), p. 220.

[17]Lewis, *George MacDonald: An Anthology,* p. xxxiii.

[18]C.S. Lewis, *Out of the Silent Planet* (New York: Macmillan, 1965), p. 73.

[19]C.S. Lewis, *Perelandra* (New York: Macmillan, 1965), p. 42.

[20]Ibid., p. 48.

Chapter Seven

[1]The first novel, *Lord Foul's Bane,* was written by 1973. The road to publication was less easy than the nearly four million sales the novels have chalked up would indicate. Donaldson submitted a prospectus with sample

chapters to every publisher in *The Literary Market Place* from A to Z. One out of four publishers asked to see the manuscript, but it wasn't until the second time around that Lester del Ray, fantasy editor of Ballantine Books, finally saw the value of the work. See "Stephen R. Donaldson, Interview," in *Publishers Weekly* (June 27, 1980), pp. 12-13.

[2]Stephen R. Donaldson, *Lord Foul's Bane* (New York: Ballantine Books, Del-Ray, 1978), p. 11. Holt, Rinehart and Winston has issued cloth editions of each work, but I refer here to the more accessible paperback editions. Imprints for other books discussed here are *The Illearth War* (New York: Ballantine, 1978), *The Power That Preserves* (New York: Ballantine, 1978), *The Wounded Land* (New York: Ballantine, 1980). Individual volumes will be noted parenthetically by abbreviated title and page number.

[3]Stephen R. Donaldson, "Interview," *Publishers Weekly* (June 27, 1980), p. 12.
[4]Ibid.
[5]Ibid., p. 13.
[6]Marshall B. Tymn, Kenneth J. Zahorski, and Robert H. Boyer, *Fantasy Literature: A Core Collection and Reference Guide* (New York: R.R. Bowker Company, 1979), p. 74.

[7]The fact that Foul disappears, but is not destroyed, opens the way, of course, to further Covenant tales.

Index

Adams, Richard
  Watership Down 29, 31, 53, 93-98
Allegory 5-13, 28, 30-31, 34
Anagogic insight 8, 13
Anti-hero 46-47, 108-09, 112
Attebery, Brian 72
Archetype 10, 26-27
Auden, W. H. 92-93, 98

Beagle, Peter
  The Last Unicorn 53
Beast fable 31-34
Bettelheim, Bruno 2
Bevan, Edwyn 95
Blake, William 35-36
Bodkin, Maud 26
Bova, Ben 14, 15
Brombert, Victor 46-47, 72
Browning, Robert 98
Buber, Martin 28
Byron, George Gordon, Lord 46, 92

Camus, Albert 46, 92, 98
Chaucer, 32, 43
Clarke, Arthur C.
  Childhood's End 17-19
Cooper, Susan 41, 62
Cox, Harvey
  Feast of Fools 58

Dickens, Charles 35, 37-42
Donaldson, Stephen R. 103-15
Dostoevsky, Fyodor 46
Dyscatastrophe 56
Dystopia 15-21

Eliade, Mircea 21-22, 24-25
Eliot, T.S. 47, 86
Eucatastrophe 56
Exupery, Antoine de Saint
  The Little Prince 51
Frost, Robert 1
Frye, Northrop 26, 92

Gardner, John
  Grendel 4
Greene, Thomas 45

Herbert, Frank
  Dune Messiah 22-23

Heroism 44-48, 72-73, 104-05
Hoffecker, W. Andrew 17
Holman, C. Hugh 6
Huxley, Aldous
  Brave New World 16-17, 19

Jung, Carl 42, 83, 87

King Arthur 59-71, 98

Leeming, David 12
Le Guin, Ursula K. 3, 6-7, 22, 26, 29, 34, 37,
  41, 45-46, 50, 65-66, 69, 73, 81-90
  The Dispossessed 50
  The Earthsea Trilogy 34, 65-66, 69, 73,
  81-90
L'Engle, Madeleine
  A Wrinkle in Time 41
Lewis, C.S. 3, 5, 7, 8, 19, 23-25, 29, 31, 41-44,
  50, 57, 61, 68-69, 75-81, 99-101
  The Abolition of Man 24, 43
  The Chronicles of Narnia 42-44, 75-81
  The Pilgrim's Regress 31
  Preface to "Paradise Lost" 3
  The Space Trilogy 25, 61, 68-69, 100-101
Lilith 79-80
Lindsay, David
  Voyage to Arcturus 30
Lundwall, Sam J. 13, 14

Magic 17, 73-90, 111-13
MacDonald, George 99-100
Manlove, C.N. 15, 46, 50
McCaffrey, Anne
  Dragonflight 85
Miller, Walter M.
  A Canticle for Leibowitz 19-21
Moorman, Charles 21, 22
Myth 8, 21-28, 97

Naive, Naivete 29, 34-41, 82-84
Novalis, 99

The Popular Culture Association of
  America 2
Projection 14-15

Quest 47, 91-102

Rabkin, Eric 49, 50, 55

Rationalism 36-37, 57
Ready, William 7, 54
Realism 13
Romanticism 35-41, 99-101
Rose, Mark 15
de Rougemont, Denis 97
Ryals, Clyde de L. 64

Sadler, Glenn 99-100
Schakel, Peter 6
Schiller, Friedrich 36-37
Science Fiction 13-21
Scientism 17, 19
Shestov, Lev 99
Siegel, Robert
    Alpha Centauri 31, 41
Slusser, George 45-46, 83
Sophocles
    Oedipus Rex 44-45
Stewart, Mary
    The Crystal Cave 61
    The Hollow Hills 61
    The Last Enchantment 61
Suvin, Darko 13

Technology 14, 23, 94
Tennyson, Alfred, Lord 46, 62-71, 98
    Idylls of the King 62-71
Tolkien, J.R.R. 1, 3, 7, 9-12, 27, 29, 51-54, 57-
    59, 77, 93, 103
    The Hobbit 9, 27, 52-54, 93
    "Leaf by Niggle" 9-12
    Lord of the Rings 7, 57-58
    "On Fairy Stories" 51-59

Utopia 15

Walton, Evangeline 29-30, 62, 69
    The Children of Llyr 69
Wangerin, Walter 21, 32-34
    The Book of the Dun Cow 32-34
Williams, Charles
    Taliessin Through Logres 68, 70
Wordsworth, William 35

Yeats, William Butler 49